Soul Mate astrology

Soul Mate Astrology

How to Find and Keep Your Ideal Mate Through the Wisdom of the Stars

TRISH MACGREGOR

Best-selling author of *The Everything Astrology Book*

FAIR WINDS
PRESS
GLOUCESTER, MASSACHUSETTS

Text © 2004 by Trish MacGregor

First published in the USA in 2004 by
Fair Winds Press
33 Commercial Street
Gloucester, MA 01930

08 07 06   3 4 5

ISBN 1-59233-091-6

Library of Congress Cataloging-in-Publication Data available

Cover design by John Hall Design
Book design by Laura H. Couallier, Laura Herrmann Design

Printed and bound in Canada

As always,

For Rob and Megan

I'd also like to thank Paula Munier,
who gave this book a home.

Contents

CHAPTER 6: Equals, One Sign Apart 107

CHAPTER 7: Best Friends, Two Signs Apart 125

CHAPTER 8: Teacher, Three Signs Apart 145

CHAPTER 9: Creative Partnership, Four Signs Apart 169

CHAPTER 10: Magician, Five Signs Apart 191

CHAPTER 11: Mentor, Opposite Signs 209

CHAPTER 12: Real Life 227

APPENDIX 237

ABOUT THE AUTHOR 242

INTRODUCTION

W̲e hear the buzz words—chemistry, electricity, seduction, sparks—and for each of us, these words conjure images. But do the words really describe the essence of a great romance? Do the words explain pairings such as Bogey and Bacall? Burton and Taylor? Hammett and Hellman? Zelda and F. Scott? Cruise and Kidman? These romances, splashed across the media to become the fodder of the tabloids, the stuff of cinematic and literary history, were born in the morass of human complexities and passionate ambitions and needs. But were all these couples soul mates?

What, exactly is a soul mate? Is it simply another person who is our ideal? Is it someone with whom we're compatible? Someone we've known in other lives? Does each of us have more than one soul mate?

Regardless of how we define what a soul mate is, one thing is certain: You will recognize the person. It may not be a conscious recognition, the kind of thing where you run over to your best friend's house, screaming that you've met your soul mate. But you'll *feel* it, some deep inner resonance that goes well beyond sparks and chemistry. You may not be able to explain it to anyone else, you may not even be able to explain it to yourself. But at some level, you'll *know*.

It may be that your soul mate is your son. Or your best friend. Or your best friend's husband or wife. It may be that your soul mate is one of your parents. But for the purpose of this book, we're talking about soul mate in terms of a romantic relationship, regardless of whether one of you is married. Or both of you are married—to other people. And before you read any further, let's define another aspect of soul mate—there isn't just one for each of us. There are many.

When astrologers read charts, many of them do so with the belief that the life we are living now is not the only life we've had, that the soul has been here many times before and will be here many times in the future. At a spiritual level, the soul as we know it in *this* life holds the memories of our other lives, and this knowledge is reflected in the birth chart. Every astrologer has his or her own way of reading past lives in a birth chart, but the only way to know whether it's accurate is if the information you're given resonates for you at an intuitive level.

Even then, the specifics probably elude you. Were you a king, a servant, an idiot savant? If you want to know the specifics, then there are other ways to explore—through past-life regression, dreams, a psychic. A birth chart won't give you the year, the place, the person you were then. In fact, that information is valuable only in that it alerts you to possible patterns you may have brought forward into this life.

Besides, the irony of all this is that quantum physics tells us that time, as we know it—past, present, future—is an illusion, that all time is simultaneous, that all time is happening *in this instant.* So at this very moment, you may be living a life in thirteenth-century France, in America of 2004, and in some other country in 2121. Different bodies, different times, but the same soul. You can see how this can become confusing very quickly. So let's deal with *this* life.

As an astrologer, I feel that the birth chart is a blueprint that reflects choices we—our souls, our higher selves—made before we were born into our current lives. We chose our parents, the conditions, the place, and the culture into which we were born, and we chose the time. In short, our souls made selections based on what it needed to grow and evolve and achieve a specific purpose. We even set up encounters, events, and situations with other souls—with their full consent—but whether we honor these predestined appointments is entirely up to us. Free will always prevails.

Recently, someone asked me whether I practiced Vedic astrology. I don't. I've resisted because it doesn't leave much room for free will. To me, a birth horoscope is a blueprint of *potential*. Nothing is cast in stone. If a client asks me whether he's going to be rich or successful, I might see the potential for wealth or success, but nothing is guaranteed. After all, part of why we're here is to learn how to fulfill our potential through our own efforts.

The soul doesn't operate in a vacuum any more than we do as physical beings. Our purpose always involves people we have known in other lives. We have debts to repay, rewards to reap, love to offer and receive and experience. It's like some massive Shakespearean play. Our roles change from life to life. Your brother in medieval France is your father in this life. Your sister during the days of the American frontier is now your boss. Your spouse in Atlantis is now your daughter. It gets weird. But one way or another, the soul works out its karma.

More often than not, we each have soul mates with whom we connect. It may be a brief fling, a guy you meet through friends, a woman you meet at work. You come together, you recognize each other—and then you move on. Maybe that's all it's meant to be. But soul mates also connect in enduring relationships—in families, in business, and romantic partnerships. Most of us seem to look for a soul mate in romance. Gay or straight, black or white, Asian or American or green people from Mars, we're looking for our other halves.

Even if we find our other half, it's no guarantee that life will unfold like a Disney movie. Happy endings aren't guaranteed. My first fiction editor was a gay man who hailed from Alabama. A Virgo. An absolute prince. The last four or five years of his life were spent with a man who had a Ph.D. and was a big deal in the Manhattan art world. No question that these two were soul mates who had chosen to come together at a particular time in history, within a particular context that would serve their souls in some way.

When AIDS rendered Chris's lover deaf, blind, and half mad, Chris flew to Minnesota nearly every weekend to be with him. And when Bill died, a part of Chris went with him, and less than two years later, AIDS took him as well. He was barely forty. To people on the outside, it smacked of tragedy. But in the cosmic scheme of things, who's to say? How can anyone on the outside define what soul purpose their relationship served for both partners?

My sense is that we live in a multidimensional universe. We make a choice, our lives go in one direction. But a part of us, of our soul, goes off in that probable direction and lives out that probable life. Imagine it. For every decision you make in your life—and to simplify it somewhat let's narrow it to major decisions about relationships—there's a you that lives out Robert Frost's "The Road Not Taken." It makes for a crowded universe and gets complicated very quickly. But it also gives you some idea of the sheer number of possibilities for soul mates.

Last year, I spoke at a local romance writers' luncheon. At the end of it, a woman came up to me who looked familiar. I knew her face, but couldn't place her name. "Do you remember me?" she asked.

And suddenly I did. We had been roommates when I was in graduate school and she was in college. It had been thirty years. We stood in the lobby for a while with several other people and tried to catch up on the past three decades. I felt a profound debt to this woman because she had introduced me to a book that changed my life—*Seth Speaks,* by Jane Roberts. I even mentioned the book and thanked her for it—thirty years late—and she smiled her Scorpio smile and said, "I always knew you would end up writing and married to your soul mate."

And right then, I realized that we are living our personal myths, that the people we hate or love or revere are the archetypes of that myth. They are the wise old men and women, the young fools, the village idiots, the lovers, the forsaken, the knights, the saviors, the warriors, the messengers. I knew that by choosing to be here now, in the early part of the twenty-first century, we have become the heroes and heroines of our personal myths and are embarked on a quest. Our grail is to *connect* in a way that is personally meaningful with people whom we have known before, in numerous guises. We connect—and then we write the script, based on the choices we make *this* time around.

Pretty simple, right?

USING THIS BOOK

Every astrologer has his or her own way of determining the deeper soul connections between a couple. One day in the gym, I got into a conversation with a guy who told me he'd seen an astrologer in Miami who had blown him away. "She told me what happened to me when I was four. She told me about my relationship with my father. With my sister...."

"How did she do this?" I asked, feeling like a medieval alchemist pursuing some esoteric knowledge.

He thought a moment, then shrugged. "Beats me. I'm an accountant."

But he was an accountant who, like some newly initiated shaman, had glimpsed the truths of a deeper reality and had begun a quest. He didn't know where he was going and, much of the time, he didn't know why he was headed in a particular direction. But that didn't seem to matter. Intuitively, he knew that the astrologer had provided him with tools, had awakened a part of his mind that had been asleep, and he was eager to explore and to go wherever the search led him. This book is something like that.

In here, you'll find two elements of a birth chart—Sun signs and the Nodes of the Moon. The Nodes aren't planets. They're points formed by the Moon's orbit around the Earth that intersect with the Earth's path around the Sun. They're always separated by 180 degrees and form an axis of energy. So if your North Node is in Cancer, your South Node is in Capricorn, the sign that is 180 degrees or six signs away from Cancer.

The South Node symbolizes our comfort zone, the accretion of traits, attitudes, and habits that we bring into this life from other lives or—if you don't believe in reincarnation—that are laid down in early childhood. The North Node symbolizes the direction we should move toward in this life to fulfill our potential and evolve spiritually. In a sense, it's the soul's agenda for *this* life.

The angle or aspect that your Sun sign or Node makes to your partner's Sun sign or Node defines the type of soul mate relationship that you have. It defines the prevalent theme: lovers, equals, best friends, teacher/student, creative partnership, magician, or mentor. One way to test these themes and categories is to apply them to people with whom you're close—a child, parent, sister or brother, a close friend—and see how the themes fit that relationship. If you find that you and your daughter share conjunctions (the lover theme) between your Suns and North Nodes, it obviously doesn't mean that you're lovers. It refers to the emotions, the psychological support, the rapport that you share, and your similarity in perceptions.

Here are the categories that go along with the seven major aspects or angles that signs and planets make to each other:

Conjunction—Lovers (same signs, 0 degrees of separation)
Semisextiles—Equals (one sign apart, 30 degrees of separation)
Sextiles—Best Friends (two signs apart, 60 degrees of separation)
Square—Teacher/Student (three signs apart, 90 degrees of separation)
Trine—Creative Partnership (four signs apart, 120 degrees of separation)
Quincunx—Magician (five signs apart, 150 degrees of separation)
Opposition—Mentor (opposite signs, 180 degrees of separation)

These seven categories describe the relationship of the twelve signs to each other and the relationship between you and your partner's Sun signs and North Nodes.

In aspects between you and your partner's respective Sun signs, the theme describes how you and your partner relate to each other in your relationship. For aspects between your Sun signs and Nodes, the descriptions illustrate your karmic path as a couple, your strengths, and your potential challenges. At the risk of repeating myself, these two elements are just a snapshot. To get a deeper and more genuine take on compatibility between couples, it's necessary to compare their entire birth charts. The signs and house placements of the Moons, Ascendants, and planets, as well as the angles these planets all make to each other, provide the full hologram.

GETTING THE MOST
FROM THIS MATERIAL

Everything you need to work with this material is included in the book. In the appendix you'll find a listing for the signs of the North Node of the Moon from 1900 to 2020, and in the first chapter you'll find the appropriate dates for each Sun sign.

Even though you don't need your birth chart or that of your partner to use this information, it's to your advantage to have it. You can get a free chart online at **www.astro.com** or at **www.astrology.com**. The more precise the birth chart, the more exact and useful this information will be. You'll need your date of birth, your birthplace, and the exact time—preferably from a birth certificate. If you don't have access to the Internet at home, then head to your nearest library, get on the Internet, and discover your chart and that of your partner. If you get into a bind and can't find the information, contact me at **www.booktalk.com/t.j.macgregor.**

In the event that you want to find out which themes apply in your relationships with other people in your life—your parents, kids, teachers, friends—these same descriptions can be used because the themes are primarily psychological.

Let's get started. Turn to the appendix, locate the time span that includes your birth date, and find the sign of your North Node. Jot it in the space below. Then glance down at the chart that shows which sign is opposite. That will be the sign of your South Node. Write that down, too.

My North Node ☊   **My South Node** ☋

Cancer   _Capricorn_

TABLE 1: **OPPOSITE SIGNS**

Your Sun Sign	Opposite
♈ Aries	♎ Libra
♉ Taurus	♏ Scorpio
♊ Gemini	♐ Sagittarius
♋ Cancer	♑ Capricorn
♌ Leo	♒ Aquarius
♍ Virgo	♓ Pisces

Now turn to the first chapter and let's explore Astrology 101.

PART
1

YOUR BLUEPRINT

"The basic principle of astrology is that man can choose to develop his good and constructive qualities... and that he can choose his times for action..."

—Grant Lewi, astrologer

ASTROLOGY 101

Romance. Just think about it for a moment. What, exactly, does it mean to you? What kinds of images does the word conjure?

In our modern world, romance seems to be the engine that runs popular culture. In *Bridget Jones' Diary*, being half of a pair is the goal. In *Kate and Leopold*, Meg Ryan finds true love and happiness with a man from another century. In *The Thorn Birds*, a priest finds love in the arms of a woman he has known since she was four or five years old. In *Cold Mountain*, Nicole Kidman and Jude Law pine for each other the entire movie, only to consummate their love toward the end of the film. Chemistry. Sparks. Electricity. No telling when or where it's going to happen.

But once it happens, astrology can help explain why it happened and whether the relationship will survive the initial attraction. It can describe the overall tone of the relationship, its creative and spiritual qualities, its sexuality and compatibility, its heart, its raw potential. Beyond that, it's all up for grabs. Beyond that, we are individuals with free will, and just because a couple has the potential for something extraordinary doesn't necessarily mean they'll live happily ever after, even if they're soul mates. Only their combined wills can do that. But to be informed is to understand how will and potential work together to create what you want in romance and in life.

In the 1969 film *John and Mary*, based on the book by the same name, Dustin Hoffman and Mia Farrow play a couple who meet in a New York bar and spend the night together. The next morning, they begin to get to know each other without ever learning each other's names. In the book, the perspectives switch back and forth between his and hers, each of them bringing very different perceptions to what's going on. By the end of the weekend, they have fallen in love and finally introduce themselves.

Chances are, John and Mary had one or several astrological contacts. Chances are that you and your partner do, too.

Ever since my daughter was old enough to understand what astrology is, I've half-jokingly remarked that before she gets married, she should give me the man's birthdate, place, and exact time of birth so that I can do his horoscope and compare it to hers. From this comparison, I will be able to tell more than she'll want me to know about the nature of their relationship. I do this already with her closest friends; they love it because it's about them. But for me, it provides insight into their friendship.

And insight is what you're after in an intimate relationship. Who is this person really? What's actually going on?

YOUR SUN SIGN

Several years ago, my husband and I rented a movie that had been out on video for some time, but which I had resisted renting or seeing because I didn't like the title. *The Gladiator.* Just the word "gladiator" conjured visions of guys in ancient Rome, fighting lions or each other or both, going at it with such macho fury that I figured, why bother? The evening news is filled with enough blood and gore and depressing stuff.

But by the end of the movie, I'd been swept up by the energy of the story and was cheering for Russell Crowe and the indomitable human spirit. As an astrologer, I knew there was only one sign that would fit this movie: Aries, the Warrior. Ironically, Crowe himself is an Aries.

This doesn't mean that every Aries was a gladiator in a past life or is destined to be a General George Patton. It does mean, though, that the Aries archetype includes passion, independence, dynamic action, and a pioneering spirit that insists on his right to live his life on his own terms and that fights to love and be loved on his terms.

Every Sun sign has an archetype, a particular signature or cluster of traits that defines it in a broad sense.

Take a look at Table 2 to find out what yours is.

TABLE 2: ROMANTIC SIGNATURES

Sign		Date	Signature
♈	Aries	March 21–April 19	independent, passionate, pioneer
♉	Taurus	April 20–May 20	sensuous, stubborn, determined
♊	Gemini	May 21–June 21	communicator, networker, versatile
♋	Cancer	June 22–July 22	nurturer, intuitive, emotional
♌	Leo	July 23–August 22	actor, warmth, generous
♍	Virgo	August 23–Sept. 22	perfectionist, analytical, inner critic
♎	Libra	Sept. 23–Oct. 22	artist, harmonizer, seeker of balance
♏	Scorpio	Oct. 23–Nov. 21	investigator, researcher, sexual, secretive
♐	Sagittarius	Nov. 22–Dec. 21	seeker, philosopher, spiritual
♑	Capricorn	Dec. 22–Jan. 19	achiever, organized, focused
♒	Aquarius	Jan. 20–Feb. 18	individualist, rebel, humanitarian
♓	Pisces	Feb. 19–March 20	mystical, imaginative, healer

These signatures are based on the ways that Sun signs are classified in terms of elements (fire, earth, air, and water) and qualities (cardinal, fixed, mutable). Both classifications have much to do with compatibility. The first classification describes the fundamental characteristic of the sign—its energy—and the second classification describes attitudes and the way you use your energy.

Take Nicole Kidman, for instance, a Gemini. That makes her a mutable air sign. Her versatility (Gemini) is most evident in the types of characters she has played—everything from Virginia Woolf in *The Hours*, for which she won an Oscar, to a wild and unpredictable witch in *Practical Magic*, to an emotionally rigid mother in the eerie movie *The Others*, to the doctor and love interest of Tom Cruise in *Days of Thunder*. Her flexibility and ability to adapt to change (mutable qualities) are apparent in the way she rebounded after her highly publicized divorce from Tom Cruise. Some pundits predicted that her career would tank; instead, her career took off.

THE QUALITIES

Cardinal signs—*Aries, Cancer, Libra,* and *Capricorn*—are outgoing and social and have initiative, drive, and motivation. They tend to move in a singular, focused way, like a horse wearing binders. They act quickly, often take on more than their share of responsibility, and get along just fine until something happens that doesn't fit into their pattern or way of doing things.

All cardinal signs are innovators, but their methods differ. Aries insists on living his life in his way, according to his code. Cancer hones in on a singular path that satisfies her emotional depths. Libra's focus is on relationships. Capricorn takes her life experiences and weaves them into practical ambitions.

Fixed signs—*Taurus, Leo, Scorpio,* and *Aquarius*—are tenacious, stubborn, and relentless in their pursuit of what they want. They're firm and sometime rigid in their beliefs and opinions. They have great persistence and determination and are extremely self-reliant. They don't adapt well to change but can generally be relied upon to honor their obligations and commitments.

The fixed nature of these signs is a current that runs through each of them, but the expression differs. Taurus digs in his heels and refuses to budge. Leo emotes. Scorpio pierces the camouflage. Aquarius busts through the status quo.

Mutable signs—*Gemini, Virgo, Sagittarius,* and *Pisces*—are adaptable and flexible. Like the chameleon, they are able to blend into their surroundings if it suits them. They can be so changeable at times, flowing with the mood of whoever or whatever is around them, that they lose sight of who they are.

The flexibility of mutable signs manifests itself uniquely for each sign. Gemini is mentally flexible. Virgo is creatively flexible. Sagittarius's adaptability lies in action, in doing. Pisces is emotionally flexible.

FIRE SIGNS

In Jean Auel's brilliant book, *Cave of the Clan Bear,* one of the most moving scenes is when the protagonist discovers how to make fire. You suddenly realize that without the discovery of fire, we would be stuck in the Stone Age. Ayla, Auel's female protagonist, is most certainly a fire sign, the pioneers of the zodiac, the movers and shakers, the activists and doers.

The **fire** signs—*Aries, Leo,* and *Sagittarius*—are independent, active, and aggressive. They are leaders who are charismatic and charming, rarely doubting their own self-worth. These individuals are dynamic, the sort of people around whom others gather. They may not have any more answers than the rest of us, but because they are often powerful speakers with charismatic personalities, they come across as leaders. Bill Clinton, a Leo, is a good example.

Aries is terrific at launching new projects and ideas but may not finish what he starts. He can be impatient and short-tempered, but he rarely holds a grudge. His passion is dramatic, fiery, and temperamental. In romance, he needs someone who is as independent as he is.

Leo is dramatic, warm-hearted, and often generous to a fault with her time and money, and when she loves, she does so completely. But she expects the same kind of unconditional love in return and must always be recognized for her accomplishments.

Sagittarius is fun-loving, philosophical, athletic, nomadic, and often deeply spiritual, but he can also be a bombastic braggart, a know-it-all who refuses to listen to other viewpoints. He's a seeker who often samples many different kinds of spiritual beliefs, usually has tremendous charm, and is tough to pin down in romantic relationships.

On a strictly superficial level, fire signs are most compatible with air signs and other fire signs.

Famous fire signs: Vincent van Gogh (Aries); Madonna (Leo); and Shirley Jackson, author of *The Haunting of Hill House* (Sagittarius).

EARTH SIGNS

The **earth** signs—*Taurus, Virgo,* and *Capricorn*—cultivate, build, and consolidate. They are practical, analytical, grounded, and efficient in all that they do. While a fire sign may be the pioneer, the earth sign brings it all down to a level the rest of us can understand. The earth sign asks, "How can I use this? Is it practical? Is it efficient?"

Imagine the New York City marathon, a race of twenty-six miles. At the beginning, the fire signs are well ahead of the pack, zipping along like there's no tomorrow. But it's the earth signs who finish the race. They may not break any speed records, but at the end of the day, they crawl across that finish line, panting, sweaty, but by God, they made it.

Taurus is pragmatic, yet often deeply mystical, and certainly one of the most stubborn signs in the zodiac. Never argue with a Taurus; you won't change his mind and, before the argument is done, you may have changed your mind. He is fixed in his opinions and his loyalties. In romance, Taurus is a sensuous romantic.

Virgo is the analyst, an extreme perfectionist in some area of her life, and a whiz when it comes to details. She can be overly critical of herself and others, which can be her undoing. She's good at using what's available, can adapt at a moment's notice to whatever the situation calls for, and has an inner core that may seem untouchable. And within that core, she's busy working on perfecting herself. In romance, she can be unpredictable, but once you've won her mind, her heart is yours.

Capricorn is the achiever, a builder who constructs his life and creative pursuits one goal at a time, always cautious and methodical, but his materialism can be his downfall. Capricorns can be as secretive as Scorpios, but for different reasons. They often build a shell around their hearts that's tough to penetrate, but once you've won their hearts, they're unerringly faithful.

On the most basic level, earth signs get along best with other earth signs and with water signs.

Some famous earth signs: George Lucas (Taurus); Stephen King (Virgo); J.R.R. Tolkien (Capricorn).

AIR SIGNS

The **air** signs—*Gemini, Libra,* and *Aquarius*—are networkers and communicators. They perceive all their life experiences through their minds. They are excited by ideas, people, and theories. While fire signs pioneer and earth signs lay down roots, air signs connect people and information. The five interrogatives belong to them: What? How? Where? Why? Who?

Gemini acquires, uses, and communicates information. She is versatile but often fickle in her affections, flexible but sometimes too flexible, and often so adaptable that she blends completely into her surroundings. As one of the two signs represented by a pair of something (twins), Gemini has a dilemma in romance that always comes down to whether the grass is greener elsewhere.

Libra seeks harmony and balance in everything he does and has a finely developed aesthetic sense. His sphere is relationships, where he's adept at seeing many sides of an issue. But the very qualities that Libra seeks often elude him personally. He's often too willing to do anything to keep the peace. He, too, can be fickle in his affections, but he may not tell you about it because Libra can't stand to hurt anyone else's feelings.

Aquarius is the individualist of the zodiac, the rebel, the paradigm buster, and also the humanitarian, the voice of the masses. Like Gemini, she's a consummate communicator and networker and usually has a vast web of friends and acquaintances. Like Taurus, she has fixed beliefs and opinions and won't buy into a belief system just because someone else says it's true. In romance, her mind must be seduced first. Once that happens, she tends to be a loyal partner.

On a basic level, air signs are most compatible with other air signs and with fire signs.

Famous air signs: Paul McCartney (Gemini); Catherine Zeta-Jones (Libra); John Travolta (Aquarius).

WATER SIGNS

Water signs—*Cancer, Scorpio,* and *Pisces*—perceive life through their emotions and intuition. They are right-brained, enigmatic, and often inscrutable, possess enormous compassion, and can be quite secretive. They are deeply attuned to inner, psychic qualities in life and in their own experiences. The lens through which they view the world is primarily subjective, and their feelings can be easily hurt.

Cancer is protective, nurturing, and deeply emotional. Her home isn't just her castle. Her home is everything, and it doesn't matter whether the actual abode is a trailer, an RV, a cabin in the wilderness, an estate, or an apartment. In fact, it isn't unusual for a Cancer to have several homes. Many of them are geniuses with real estate investments. When it comes to affairs of the heart, however, Cancer can be cagey, moving the way a crab moves if confronted with a sticky emotional situation.

Scorpio digs, penetrates, and pierces the camouflage of whatever he touches. He's after the absolute bottom line. He's the transformer of the zodiac. He breaks taboos, he's intense, and yes, if you cross him, he may hold a grudge. Before you can win a Scorpio's heart, you have to win his trust. And that can be a difficult thing, for sure.

Pisces imagines, intuits, and feels her way through life with such depth that most of us don't have a clue what really goes on inside her. She may miss seeing the trees in the forest, but she definitely sees the forest. She's more right-brained than left-brained, and she never makes apologies for it. She's one of two signs represented by a pair of something—two fish—and this points to a natural ambivalence in her nature that can become an issue in relationships. Sometimes, she's at war with herself—her head says do one thing, her heart screams for her to do another. Pisces has the capacity to heal whatever she touches. She's a sucker for a sob story, though, and runs the risk of becoming either a victim or a savior.

Water signs are most compatible with other water signs and with earth signs.

Famous water signs: Tom Hanks (Cancer); Bill Gates (Scorpio); Liz Taylor (Pisces).

THE LANGUAGE OF ASTROLOGY

Every language begins with an alphabet, and astrology is no exception. Its alphabet isn't your typical ABCs, but it's the same idea. It's called the planets.

Every sign is ruled by a planet, and that planet's nature—much of it defined by mythology—colors the meaning of the sign. Take Aries, ruled by Mars. In mythology, Ares is the god of war. He rules the military, guns, and violence. He's depicted as a ruthless god, eaten up by his own passions and power. Of course, we're talking about ancient Rome and Greece, when life was brutal, stripped down to its bare essentials. Think *The Gladiator, Spartacus, Braveheart.* In our modern world, the analogy would be 9/11, the invasion of Afghanistan and Iraq, and the Bush administration's foreign policy. Attack—and ask questions later.

This doesn't mean that if you're born under the sign of Aries you're a warmonger. But in some facet of your life, you're a fighter.

How about Mercury? In mythology, he was known as Hermes, the winged messenger of the gods. It makes sense, then, that Mercury rules communication and travel. It also rules the conscious mind, logic, and reasoning. Its rulership, then, of Gemini, the communicator, certainly fits, and so does its rulership of analytical Virgo. Both signs think fast, and Gemini also moves quickly, restlessly, rather like Hermes did. You get the idea here. Your sign takes on the qualities of the planet that rules it.

In the days before the outer planets—Uranus, Neptune, and Pluto— were discovered—there was a major problem with rulership because the math didn't add up. There were twelve signs and, counting the Sun and Moon, only seven planets. That meant that some planets ruled more than one sign. Even when the outer planets were discovered and the rulerships were shuffled around, these signs were considered to be co-ruled by the traditional planets.

Mars, for example, used to rule both Aries and Scorpio; Jupiter ruled both Sagittarius and Pisces; and Saturn ruled both Capricorn and Aquarius. These co-rulers are still used today to further describe the respective signs. Even with the discovery of the outer three planets, the math problem persisted, which is why Gemini and Virgo are both ruled by Mercury, and Taurus and Libra are both ruled by Venus.

In Table 3, the traditional rulerships are in parentheses.

TABLE 3: RULERSHIPS

Planet	Rules	Represents
☉ Sun	♌ Leo	Essence and energy of life, where and how you shine, self-expression, ego, yang energy, father, husband
☽ Moon	♋ Cancer	Emotions, intuition, what makes you feel secure, yin energy, mother
☿ Mercury	♊ Gemini ♍ Virgo	Intellect, conscious mind, communication, travel, the left brain, writing, contracts
♀ Venus	♉ Taurus ♎ Libra	Love life, romance, beauty, wife, women, art
♂ Mars	♈ Aries (Scorpio)	Physical and sexual energy, determined
♃ Jupiter	♐ Sagittarius (Pisces)	Luck, creativity, success, prosperity, growth, expansion
♄ Saturn	♑ Capricorn (Aquarius)	Rules of physical existence, responsibility, discipline, limitations and restrictions
♅ Uranus	♒ Aquarius	Individuality, genius, eccentricity, originality
♆ Neptune	♓ Pisces	Illusions, higher inspiration, mysticism, escapism
♇ Pluto	♏ Scorpio	Profound transformation, what's hidden, the underworld, power, death, sex
Nodes		Points, not planets. The North Node ☊ represents the direction we should move toward in this life to fulfill our potential, and the South Node ☋ represents habits and attitudes accrued in past lives that we should release.

THE HEART AND SOUL OF YOUR SUN SIGN

S everal years ago, my husband, daughter, and I went to Ecuador on vacation. Thanks to the Internet, we were able to plan everything in advance, and one of the places we chose to visit was the city of Banos, which lies in a valley in the Andes. Our lodging was at the Hacienda Manteles, which had a great Web site that seemed to feature everything we were looking for—spectacular scenery, horseback riding, hiking, and great native food, and it boasted nearly thirty types of hummingbirds. It was close to the city of Banos, and we figured we would be able to walk into town.

Wrong.

The hacienda sat on a plateau near the top of a peak and the only way to get there was on a steep and winding road that had no guardrails. Look to your right or left, and the land fell away and plunged several thousand feet straight down. Fortunately, the hacienda employed a charming bilingual guide named Diego.

On the day that Diego drove us into Banos, I was sitting in the front seat of the car and I happened to ask him what he was doing stuck on a mountaintop in the middle of nowhere, and he laughed and told me a strange story. Several years before, he had been working for an oil company and was sent into the jungle to do some work. The heat was almost unbearable, the living conditions were deplorable, and he hated it.

Then one afternoon he was out hiking and found a young Indian boy who had collapsed on the ground of the jungle and was unconscious. Diego knew the kid was a member of a small, native tribe that had kept moving deeper into the jungle as civilization encroached, eating up their world. He took the boy to the oil camp and nursed him back to health. When the boy was finally better, he left without ever having spoken a word to Diego.

Several months later, Diego was out hiking again and was bitten by a snake. He knew the snake was poisonous, but before he could do anything to help himself, he blacked out. He came to three days later, with the kid he had helped standing over him. The boy had found Diego and because Diego had helped him, the tribe now saved Diego's life. They had called in their shaman, who had treated his snakebite with native remedies and herbs.

"I know I should have died from that snakebite. But there I was, alive after three days in a coma."

He subsequently spent two years living with the tribe (and never went back to work for the oil company), learning their traditions, their healing methods, and their language. By the time he rejoined civilization, he was no longer the same man who had gone into the jungle two years earlier. He got a job as a guide at the hacienda and began to write a book about his experiences. A Spanish publisher had expressed interest in the book but wanted to know the exact location of the tribe. Diego refused to divulge it. He had promised the tribe that he would never reveal where they lived.

Those two years had not only changed his life but also completely opened him up to everything that was mystical, strange, and inexplicable according to existing belief systems.

When he finished his story, I asked if he was a Taurus. He looked shocked. "How did you know that?"

I knew because he talked like a man who had connected with the mystical undercurrents so intrinsic to Taurus. It's rarely obvious in Taurus, probably because this sign is one of the most taciturn, not given to quick confidences or an exchange of secrets. But the quality is there, like a facet of a gem that must be turned in a certain way toward the light before its full beauty is obvious. His stubborn refusal to divulge the location of the tribe, his adherence to a promise, almost smacked of Taurus. It helped, too, that I've been married to a Taurus for twenty years!

Every Sun sign has qualities that lie at the heart of what the sign is really about. If you listen to what people say, observe them, note their interests and passions, even their appearance, the qualities of the sign suddenly seem obvious. And that's what we're after here, the bottom line for each Sun sign. Once you have it, then it's easy to understand what that sign is looking for in a soul mate relationship.

♈

THE ARIES HEART AND SOUL

Whether you're male or female, your bottom line is excitement. It's the itch you can't reach, the fuel of your impatience and restlessness, and the urge that propels you forward to embrace new experiences. It's also why you probably enjoy competitive sports—perhaps as a player, but also as a spectator. Either way, it's the thrill that grabs you.

As a cardinal fire sign, it's the thrill that seizes you when you're in the throes of a new romance. You enjoy the challenge, the seduction, the passion. The frenetic pace of a new romance infuses your senses, making you feel more alive and powerful. Then the dust settles, the frenzy ebbs, and you're in the midst of a relationship where certain things are expected of you within the context of ordinary, daily life. That's when the trouble starts. Boredom. Restlessness. Futility. So you walk away, already on the prowl again, not suspecting that you may have deserted your soul mate.

You argue, of course, that your soul mate wouldn't be any less exciting than you are. That may be true, but it's also true that Aries is great at initiating, but not so great at follow-through and commitment. Blinded by your need for excitement, you may miss the opportunity of a lifetime.

Nowhere is it written, after all, that a soul mate is your clone. And, also, let's face it: You're impatient. You get into a new romance and you want everything to zip along at the speed of light. When it doesn't, you're taken aback.

So the next time you're caught up in the thrill of a new romance, Aries, look beneath the surface. Get a feel for who your partner is minus the trappings. Use your intuition to probe your own emotions. Does this relationship feel different than others? Is there something about it that resonates in the deeper core of your being?

THE TAURUS HEART AND SOUL

Some astrologers contend that your sign is ruled by the Earth rather than by Venus, and there's certainly good reason for the argument. You're a nature lover, probably a consummate gardener, and you have an innate feel for the land—its beauty, its mystery, its timelessness. You're as stolid and dependable as the Earth, too, and rarely reveal yourself too quickly. It isn't that you're distrustful, merely reticent, with a genuine need for privacy.

Beneath your quiet exterior, however, lies a mystic in the making. Your exploration of cosmic mysteries may be one of the driving forces in your life, even if you don't realize that yet. Your fascination, though, isn't that of a full-fledged believer. You're skeptical but open-minded, always seeking to make the esoteric practical and useful to yourself and others.

With the Venus rulership, you're a sensualist, and that sensuality extends to every area of your life—from the foods you eat to the vacations you take to your sexual tastes. You enjoy being surrounded by beautiful things, but you usually aren't a collector, as Capricorn might be, and you don't like clutter. You prefer tasteful art, tasteful music, tasteful foods, and tasteful people. Thanks to Venus, you recognize class when you see it.

Generally, you're attracted to people who share your values, interests, and passions—but then, isn't that true of most of us? Due to the fixed earth nature of your sign, though, you may discount partners who seem to be too different from you.

Before you discount any potential partner, Taurus, make sure that you've done more than scratch the surface of who that person is. Dive in. Investigate that other person's inner world. You can never be sure how your soul mate is disguised this time around.

♊
THE GEMINI HEART AND SOUL

Over the years, I've read many descriptions of Gemini as being flighty, flaky, and fickle—not just in the romance department, but in life generally. You're also supposed to be superficial and incapable of maintaining a relationship for more than five minutes, craving unpredictability and excitement as a regular diet. Well, as a Gemini, I beg to differ. Yes, Geminis have moments of flightiness, flakiness, and fickleness—but probably no more than any other sign. Yes, they like excitement, and routine is as anathema to them as it is to an Aries or a Sagittarius. But please, to say that we can't love anyone for longer than five minutes?

As an air sign, you live in your head, Gemini, and since you're represented by the twins, it means that much of the time you're of two minds. These two minds (and personalities) may not always want the same thing or be seeking the same kinds of traits in a partner. This can be a problem, but it isn't insurmountable. After all, we're not talking schizophrenia, simply a difference in opinion.

Your romantic interests tend toward people who seduce your mind. But what about the rest of you? Should you immediately dismiss the partner who loves to camp and fish? And what about the partner who enjoys things that don't appeal to you? It's possible that you and your soul mate contracted to be teachers to each other this time around, and part of that teaching may involve experiences in new areas.

On the other hand, your soul mate may be working in the same area that you do, but in a different way. Or he or she may be working in an allied field. It behooves you to nurture and develop your intuition and develop a solid idea of who you are and what you're looking for so that when that camper enthusiast or avid fisherman comes along, you'll recognize him or her.

And oh, Gemini, one other thing: Don't worry about the twin stuff. Forget what other people say. You feel comfortable inhabiting two skins at the same time and, besides, they serve a purpose. While one twin is engaged in raucous behavior, the other is quietly observing, absorbing, listening. It's a good disguise.

THE CANCER HEART AND SOUL

As the most subjective of the signs, you probably won't need a whole lot of guidelines about recognizing your soul mate. You're exceptionally intuitive; some of you are downright psychic. So recognition isn't the challenge, but trust may be.

You want very much to trust your partner, but you dislike sticky emotional situations and discussions. When you're put on the spot about an emotional issue, it's likely that you dodge the subject altogether. Like the crab that symbolizes your sign, you skitter sideways. In fact, if you live near the ocean, head down to the shore some afternoon and observe the behavior and motion of crabs. Notice how they desert one shell and slide into another. Their homes aren't just their castles; they are protection as well. That's pretty much how you feel about your home, too, so before you bring a potential partner into your most private sanctuary, trust is vital.

As a cardinal water sign, your emotions are the most powerful force in your life. You love deeply and crave a mutually loving relationship. But it isn't easy for a potential partner to break through the shell around your heart. So, Cancer, if you're reluctant to let a potential partner into your life, your home, and your heart, how do you know for sure whether that person is your soul mate?

This doesn't mean you should hurl open your doors to everyone who crosses your path. Instead, separate yourself from your fear, if you can, turn your considerable intuition toward each potential partner you meet, and ask yourself, What do I really feel about this person? Is there an inner resonance? If you feel intuitively that there's something worthwhile to explore in the relationship, then step out of your shell, Cancer, and stand a while beneath the sunlit sky, out in the open and unprotected.

♌
THE LEO HEART AND SOUL

Everything for you comes wrapped in high drama. Whether it's your latest relationship or your job, your kids or your most recent vacation, there's usually drama involved. Whether it's an actual drama or merely an incident that you've embellished to add flair and flamboyance to your daily life, the end result is the same. Drama is part of your natural flamboyance.

More than any other sign, you need an audience. It doesn't have to be a huge audience—one person in the coffee room will do just fine—but for many Leos, this need translates into a job in the entertainment industry. This can get you into trouble in relationships because you demand that a partner make outward expressions of his or her love for you. But let's face it, not everyone is as demonstrative as you are, Leo. And if you meet someone who is quieter than you or who moves you away from your concern with yourself, is that a reason to slam the door on the relationship?

In the larger scheme of things, your soul chose to be born this time under a Leo Sun. Perhaps the reason relates to the creative impetus of the Leo Sun or to the sign's inherent love of kids. But it's equally possible that some other reason exists for the soul's choice. So if you shut the door on someone who doesn't act in the way you expect, how do you know for sure that person isn't your soul mate?

You don't. A soul mate isn't necessarily someone who acts only as you expect him or her to act or who is here simply to complement you. Soul mates have their own agendas, too. Be sure, Leo, to check out the sign of your Nodes and the angles these make to your Sun and do the same for your partner. These pieces of information will tell you a lot about the deeper purposes not only in your own life but in that of your soul mate as well.

In other words, leave your options open.

♍
THE VIRGO HEART AND SOUL

Regardless of what you're doing in your life, who you're involved with, or what your goals and dreams are, Virgo always runs up against the wall called "Am I worthy?" Sometimes the question is phrased differently. It may be, "Can I do this?" "Am I smart enough (or pretty enough, educated enough, creative enough, or whatever) to do this?" When it comes to matters of the heart, this same self-doubt and self-criticism operates.

What people fail to understand about you, Virgo, is that you're a work in progress. As a mutable earth sign, you're flexible, adaptable, and creative. You're constantly striving toward a perfect ideal—of yourself, your loved ones, your creative and spiritual endeavors, the entire vast canvas of your life. To achieve this ideal, you turn your sharp, analytical eye on the flaws and imperfections of the raw material and find it grossly wanting. So you engage in endless dialogues with yourself, analyzing every little detail until all those details are shredded and lying in scraps on the floor. Whether you're criticizing yourself or your partner, the devastation to the relationship is the same either way.

Most Virgos enjoy their solitude. They may not crave a steady diet of it, but they can certainly amuse themselves in the absence of company. So one element you may want to take into account in any relationship is whether your partner gives you the freedom to be alone.

You're at your best when you do things for others and do it out of love or compassion rather than out of a sense of duty or obligation. Instead of critiquing any potential partner, get to know that person first. Look for the larger picture rather than focusing on the details. Use your imagination and intuition. Let your right brain do some of the work, then turn things over to your left brain to decide whether the relationship is worth pursuing.

Once you become conscious of this inner process, you won't waste time on relationships that don't feel right—and you'll recognize your soul mate when he or she enters your life.

♎

THE LIBRA HEART AND SOUL

You're the seminal romantic, in love with love. It's different for you, though, than it is for your opposite sign, Aries, because it's not so much the initial rush and thrill that seizes you, but the pervasive stars-in-your-eyes sort of feeling. The fuzzy feel-good of it all: That's what you enjoy.

It's important to you that a partner at least respect your artistic interests and passions—music, art, literature, or whatever they may be—and that he or she supports your artistic aspirations. Equally important, though, is that you don't put yourself in a position where you become the perennial peacemaker in a relationship. For a Libra, this tendency often leads to peace at any cost, and it has repercussions down the line that stifle your own creativity and intuition.

You like partners who are physically attractive and know how to romance and court you. But suppose you meet someone who isn't especially romantic but is still crazy about you? What then? Or suppose you meet someone who may not be as attractive as you want or who is more independent and feisty than you like, but who has other qualities you admire? Do you immediately write this person off?

Your soul mate can enter your life in any guise, at any point in your life, so it's important that you first know who you are independent of everyone else. Define yourself. Strive for independence. Identify your creative interests, your boundaries. Otherwise, you may fall into that Libra trap where you meld with your beloved and forget who you are.

♏
THE SCORPIO HEART AND SOUL

Take a look at the adjectives that describe your sign: intense, creative, passionate, secretive, powerful, profound, sexual, psychic, intuitive. They probably won't all fit all of the time, but at certain periods in your life, some will fit like the proverbial glove.

While each sign has its strengths, challenges, and distinctive quirks, yours is undoubtedly one of the most misunderstood. Profoundly trans-formative experiences define your life and, as a result, you live at levels that most people don't, which makes it difficult to get to know you. Trust is one of your issues. You don't give it easily. In fact, you may not give it at all—people have to earn your trust and prove their loyalty. But once they do, you allow them into your private sanctuary.

You're a fixed water sign, opinionated and sure of your opinions. You have great emotional and spiritual depth and a memory so steeped in intuition and feeling that little escapes you. In a partnership, you may be so immersed in probing what lies beneath the other person's exterior that you lose sight of the moment—its infinite beauties, its small miracles. At times, you even forget how to have fun. Find the flow of the moment and move with it rather than resisting it. Do ordinary things with your partner; discover the particular texture of how you are together. And once you feel comfortable with that, dive in for the deeper stuff.

After all, Scorpio, your soul mate may be here to remind you that even though we're spiritual beings in a physical universe, it's daily reality that makes up the substance of our lives.

THE SAGITTARIUS HEART AND SOUL

You specialize in the Big Picture, and it doesn't matter whether that picture is a philosophy, a trip, a workshop, or a relationship. You go into whatever it is with your sights on how it may expand the larger framework of your life. As a mutable fire sign ruled by Jupiter, you constantly seek to expand your knowledge, experiences, and worldview. You may not do this consciously, but it's part of the force that propels you into new experiences.

You're a seeker. Sometimes you're seeking knowledge and experience and other times you're looking for…well, good times and fun! You need a partner who not only understands that but also can keep up with you. Negative and depressed types aren't your cup of tea; your natural optimism and buoyancy couldn't stand it for more than five minutes.

In your ability to see the magnificence of the Big Picture, you run the risk of believing the Big Picture is the ultimate truth—i.e., that you hold the truth. This kind of attitude is more common in less self-aware Sagittarians. But for anyone born under this sign, there's a tendency to become close-minded about your beliefs and dismiss any potential partner who doesn't believe as you do. Big mistake. After all, suppose you're a vegetarian Buddhist and your soul mate has come disguised as a meat-eating Methodist?

Your thrust in relationships depends to a large extent on which part of the Sagittarian archetype is most prevalent in your life—nomad, adventurer, student, spiritual seeker, philosopher, politician, or publisher. With any partner, your best bet is to forget about the Big Picture until you have a strong sense of the other person and how he or she fits into your vision for your own life.

♑
THE CAPRICORN HEART AND SOUL

You're a complicated package. On the one hand, you're dedicated, hard working, studious, reserved, responsible, and practical; on the other, your libido is running wild.

Many Capricorns pour their libidinous energy into their careers, which is why Capricorn is usually associated with career ambitions. Yes, you're ambitious, you enjoy having money to spend, and your career is important to you. But if you allow your career and your materialistic concerns to subsume your chances for a satisfying sexual and emotional life, you probably will regret it. Not only that, but your soul mate may pass you by like the proverbial ship in the night and you'll never know it.

As a cardinal fixed sign, you don't like surprises. You like things laid out, as if in a neat grid or—better yet—in a fine, straight line where you can see from point A to point Z. Yet, surprises are the stuff that makes up some of life's most memorable experiences, so don't close yourself off to the new and unknown.

It's best to maintain an awareness of your emotional needs about all areas of your life. Does your career satisfy you emotionally? Is your partner emotionally responsive? What emotions does your partner kindle in you? Are your creative goals aligned with your deeper emotional needs? The closer you are to what you feel about yourself and your world, the less likely it is that you and your soul mate will fail to connect this time around.

⩓⩓
THE AQUARIUS HEART AND SOUL

You live in your mind. This can be said of fellow air signs Gemini and Libra, too, but because you're also a fixed sign, your mind is your bottom line, where everything begins and ends. Because your mind is the conduit to your emotions, it shouldn't come as any big surprise that unless a relationship speaks to your intellect, you aren't interested.

You're an independent, free-spirited person whose relationships are usually unconventional, with no strings attached. You don't need a partner to feel complete. You're interested in anyone and everyone who is offbeat or eccentric or goes against the norm in some way. You like idea people. You enjoy the ways in which ideas connect, and when the connection isn't obvious but you sense it's there, you can be as relentless as Scorpio in digging for it.

In romance, one thing is for sure: You and your partner must have an easy flow of communication for the relationship to work. Then, even if your interests lie in opposite directions, it doesn't matter because you can still talk to each other. You have a great respect for individuality and aren't threatened by it in a partner.

You lack the emotional intensity of the fire and water signs. But be prepared for that to change when your soul mate rolls into your life!

♓
THE PISCES HEART AND SOUL

Gentle, dreamy Pisces. You're always there for the people you love and it doesn't matter whether they're down and out, sick, in jail, or otherwise indisposed. This is precisely why Pisces is often depicted as both victim and savior.

Your sign is symbolized by two fish swimming in opposite directions. Just as Gemini's twins have a tough time agreeing on things, so do your fish. But with you, the dichotomy is even more pronounced. Sometimes, the fish represent your mind and your heart, with one screaming to go one way and the other screaming to go another way. Other times, the fish symbolize the spiritual heights to which you can rise—and the depths of escapism. Both extremes are due to the planet that rules your sign—Neptune.

However, your sign is co-ruled by Jupiter, which also rules Sagittarius. That rulership gives you a philosophical bent and confers a fun-loving aspect to your personality. So, sometimes the two fish may represent the respective natures of the two planets that rule your sign.

In romance, it's difficult for you to separate your considerable intuition from the whisperings of your heart. To avoid choosing the wrong partner, find a way to ground your energy—meditation, tai chi, yoga, or something similar—and then ask yourself two simple questions:

Is this relationship good for me?

Am I playing either victim or savior?

If the answer to the first is yes and the answer to the second is no, then go for it, Pisces!

THE NODES
OF THE MOON

Twenty years ago, my husband and I were writing magazine articles for a variety of publications and interviewed a woman named Renie Wiley, an artist and psychic who worked with police on criminal investigations. We had the opportunity to observe Renie on a missing child case, subsequently wrote an article about her for *Fate Magazine,* and became good friends.

Renie, a Sagittarius, was an ace astrologer, one of those self-taught people who simply has a gift for it. She became my mentor in astrology, a role that evolved from our friendship, and it was from her that I learned about the Nodes. She always emphasized that there were three levels of meanings to the Nodes—by sign, house, and aspect. In this chapter, we'll discuss the Nodes by signs and in the next chapter, by houses. Nodes by aspects, which relates to soul mates, begins with chapter five.

If you haven't done so already, look up the sign of your North Node in the ephemeris. If you were born, for instance, between January 27, 1949 and July 26, 1950, then your North Node is in Aries. Because the South Node is always in the opposite sign, your South Node would be in Libra.

(Use Table 1 in the introduction to locate the sign opposite from that of your North Node.)

♌
NORTH NODE DESCRIPTIONS

This section describes the North Node in each of the signs. Because the North and South Nodes of the Moon form an axis of energy, a kind of fulcrum, the descriptions of the North Nodes in the twelve signs is actually a distillation of both nodal meanings.

♈ IN ARIES

You're here this time around to discover and mine the riches of your genuine self. Doesn't sound like too tough a challenge, does it? It requires independence, defining your own values—as opposed to adapting the values of family or friends—and following your passions, whatever they are.

With a cardinal fire sign North Node, you'll have opportunities throughout your life to strike out on your own, to be innovative, to pioneer some new concept or belief, or to explore something (or some place) entirely new. Whether you rise to the challenge is, of course, entirely up to you. But be forewarned: It's the path that will lead you to fulfill your potential and to evolve spiritually in this lifetime.

In terms of relationships, the voice of your Libra South Node, your comfort zone, will send you off in search of the perfect partner, the elusive soul mate. There's nothing wrong with the search. After all, that's what we're talking about here, soul mates. However, it's doubtful you'll find a soul mate or a perfect partner until you've established who you are and separate from your family, your friends, and anyone else in your life who seeks to define you.

The Aries North Node blueprint is about you, not others; about your independence rather than codependence; about following your impulses rather than restraining them; about upsetting the status quo instead of keeping the peace at any cost. Once you learn these particular lessons, then you're ready to meet your soul mate and to embrace the relationship as one between equals.

So where do you start?

Seek solitude. Okay, this one will feel very uncomfortable when you start out along the Aries North Node path. Your comfort zone is screaming for you to be with other people, the more the merrier, a party every night, thank you very much. It doesn't mean you have to become a hermit, but how about five or ten minutes of meditation every day? Or maybe a weekly hike or bike ride or time at the gym is in order. Perhaps you have a hobby that you love. It doesn't matter so much what you do in solitude, as long as you do something on a regular basis.

Ignore disapproval from others. The comfort zone of the Libra South Node really dislikes disapproval from others. It's one of those internal buttons which, when pushed, is difficult to ignore. You immediately want to run around, smoothing ruffled feathers, assuring everyone that you were, well, just kidding. Whether you're sticking to goals you've set or you've quit your job or are following an impulse, the Aries North Node requires you to go through with it even if everyone in the universe tells you you're wrong. You have to depend on what feels right to you.

Be spontaneous. When you're spontaneous, you're in the flow of your own desires and are acting on those desires. Your Libra South Node will fight you on this point, will urge you to put on the brakes, to wait, to discuss things with family, partners, friends. But to fully explore, nurture, and express your individuality, it's important that when you feel the urge to do something, you do it. Follow our impulses.

The Aries/Libra axis addresses our identity, who we are as individuals, and who we are as members of a larger collective. With your Aries North Node, the challenge is to define your individuality separate from the collective, whether that collective is your family, a relationship, or the larger community in which you live. Once you learn to do that, you're able to draw on your Libra South Node for balance and harmony in all your relationships.

Examples: Neil Armstrong, Ram Dass, Florence Nightingale, Jay Leno.

♉ IN TAURUS

With a fixed earth sign North Node, you're here this time around to define your values and to find your spiritual balance through the physical senses. Your playground is the entire smorgasbord of physical reality, and you're meant to sample all of it and build something meaningful from and through your experiences. Whether you're building a house or a screenplay or a relationship, you're called upon to do so with patience, intuitive awareness, dedication, and loyalty. In other words, when you build, there aren't any shortcuts. You do the work for as long as it takes.

In a partnership, Taurus North Node often seeks a merging at the soul level, a kind of morphing where the two become one. Believe as I believe. Do as I do. This is the voice of your Scorpio South Node, your comfort zone, where you seek control and power over others. Few things can damage a relationship faster than this. If you're involved in this kind of partnership, one thing is certain: All hell will break loose when your partner rebels, demanding to be valued as an individual and not just as part of a couple.

With your Taurus North Node, you have to relinquish your need to control others before you can successfully maintain a soul mate relationship or fulfill your creative potential. Your focus should be on consciously empowering yourself through an exploration of your skills, talents, and resources. There are certain steps you can take to make this process simpler.

Dispel secrecy. Your Scorpio South Node won't like this one at all. But it's an integral part to your evolution this time around. Be open and upfront with partners about what you feel and think.

Be selfish. It sounds odd, doesn't it? Most of us are taught the opposite. But for Taurus North Node people, the selfishness revolves around self-empowerment. You must do whatever it takes to empower yourself, even when it means putting your own needs and desires first. Once you're self-empowered, you probably won't feel the need to control others.

Be patient. Your Scorpio South Node isn't the most patient node on the block! Its energy is constantly pushing you to dig deeper, probe, and investigate—and to do it fast. Part of the Taurean archetype, regardless of what planet or point it's connected with, is allowing events and emotions to unfold at their own sweet pace. The fixed earth nature of this node demands patience in order to build anything. So for you, patience really is a virtue.

Find a center of calm. Your Scorpio South Node indicates you're no stranger to crisis and profound transformation. This time around, you're supposed to find a center of calm within yourself that allows you to remain on an even keel even if the rest of the world is collapsing around you. This is one of the reasons Taurus North Node people gravitate toward nature, art, and music and tend to be physical people. It behooves you to have a regular exercise routine, to practice meditation and yoga, and to develop your creative and artistic interests. Any of these pursuits helps establish an inner center of calm.

Balance sensuality. Due to the deeply sexual nature of Scorpio and the sensuousness of Taurus, there can be a tendency toward excess with this nodal axis. Excessive sex, eating, spending, drinking, drug use…you get the idea. Musician Kurt Cobain, a heroin addict who committed suicide, is an example of this excessive sensuality.

The Taurus/Scorpio axis is about building and tearing down, growth and destruction, birth and rebirth. When you empower yourself through the development and use of your physical senses, then you're able to draw on a vast reservoir of intuitive power to become an equal partner in a soul mate relationship.

Examples: Greg Allman, Pearl Buck, Kurt Cobain, Lucille Ball.

♊ IN GEMINI

Your mission, should you choose to accept it, is to use your insatiable curiosity to gather and disseminate information. The concept itself is glaringly simple, but the ways in which you go about doing what you're here to do probably aren't simple at all. But that's okay. Gemini, one of the two signs in the zodiac symbolized by two of something, can multitask with great ease. In real life, this could mean that you combine your gift of gab with your people talents in teaching, writing, music, films, public relations, advertising, or research.

With a Sagittarius South Node, it's likely that you have a particular belief system or worldview that provides a firm foundation for your life. It allows you to compare and contrast your views with those of other people. But when you're in the comfort zone of your South Node, your natural curiosity about opposing viewpoints shuts down. You may become self-righteous or believe that your truth is the only truth and refuse even to listen to other people's ideas. It's pretty obvious how problematic this could be in a relationship where a partner holds a different viewpoint.

With this nodal axis, it's likely that there's someone in your life whose belief system is radically different than your own. It may not be a partner or spouse, but perhaps a sibling, parent, or relative. Rather than arguing with this person and trying to convince him or her that you're right, that your truth is better, look at the person as a teacher. Attempt to listen with an open mind. And remember: Each of us is here for a different purpose. If a belief system—even one that is completely different from yours—offers comfort and sustenance to the person who holds it, then what business is it of yours to demean it?

Once you become aware of this particular pattern in yourself, you can take steps to rectify it. Here are some guidelines that may help.

Be curious. Curiosity is probably your most valuable resource. Nurture it in all things, but especially in terms of other people's belief systems. If someone's worldview or beliefs push your buttons, ask yourself why. Resistance is often a clue to something within yourself that you need to explore and understand.

Listen. You may be so focused at times on what you want to say that you really don't listen to what the other person is saying. Give other people the same consideration they give you when it comes to self-expression. Everyone's story or point of view is deeply important him or her. Make sure that when you listen, you do so completely.

Believe in yourself. This area can be challenging for the Gemini North Node. Thanks to the twins that symbolize the sign, you can be moody and temperamental and often have to juggle dual needs, desires, and beliefs. While one twin whispers, "Go for it," the other twin snickers in the shadows, "Yeah? Who're you kidding?" To successfully navigate your own duality, it's necessary to believe in yourself. This doesn't mean that one day you believe and the next day you don't. It means you must develop a rock solid belief in your own abilities and talents through good times and bad.

In your eagerness to experience everything, you have a tendency to rush from one appointment or project or relationship to another. Better to savor each moment, to live it as though it may be your last.

The Gemini/Sagittarius axis is about the forest and the trees. Gemini sees the trees—the facts and trivia that make up the big picture—and Sagittarius sees the forest—the big picture. The challenge is to find the right balance between the two.

Examples: Jimmy Buffet, Rosalyn Carter, Deepak Chopra, Bill Clinton, Connie Chung.

♋ IN CANCER

This lifetime is about your emotions and your intuition. You're here to discover what makes you feel secure and to establish that base so that you can fulfill your potential. When you work from a centered place within your own feelings, your life unfolds right on track.

With a Capricorn South Node, you undoubtedly have clear goals and ambitions. However, because this is your comfort zone, you often feel a need to control everything and everyone in your life and assume a lot of responsibility. In fact, you probably feel personally responsible for things that don't have anything to do with you! You want to achieve and be recognized for your achievements and work hard to make that happen. But because these traits come from your South Node, you won't get anywhere unless you're living from a centered place within your own emotions and intuition.

You're so sensitive and intuitive about what your partner is feeling that you can see a crisis coming before it arrives and then adjust your feelings and behavior in an attempt to avert it. It's a form of control and allows you to avoid an unpleasant emotional confrontation. There are several problems with this method of control, and foremost among them is your partner's resentment when he or she catches on. And, eventually, you have to deal with the issues you're trying to avoid.

Here are some simple steps to help you navigate the Cancer North Node more smoothly.

Stay in tune with your emotions. The more aware you are of how you feel, the clearer the rest of your life will be. If you have an unpleasant or negative emotion, don't ignore it or obsess about it. Just take note of it, let it flow through you—and then release it.

Release the need for control. The only person you can control is yourself. You can control your actions and reactions, your thoughts and desires, and your home and personal environment. But you can't control what other people do or think, and the sooner you learn this lesson, the happier you'll be.

Open your heart. You probably feel that it's a sign of weakness to depend on other people or to reveal too much about your feelings. But one of the greatest strengths of the Cancer North Node is that you're more open emotionally and intuitively. It's to your advantage to look inward and tend to your inner life with the same care that you do your outer life.

The Cancer/Capricorn nodal axis is about how we live our lives in private and in public. It's about home and family versus career, right brain versus left brain, the inner world versus the outer world. Cancer North Node encourages you to let down your defenses and connect emotionally and intuitively with others.

Examples: Johann Sebastian Bach, Erma Bombeck, Daphne DuMaurier, Robert Bly.

♌ IN LEO

Lucky you! This is your lifetime for creative self-expression. You're here to learn what you truly want, how to have fun and be happy, and how to make it all happen. And along this path, you're supposed to learn how to give and receive unconditional love. Sounds pretty cool, right?

Your Aquarius South Node provides you with an awareness of group dynamics, humanitarian ideals, tolerance for people who are different than you, and a deep commitment to the belief that we are all created equal. Your comfort zone, in other words, lies in the world of ideas and abstracts rather than in the heart. You're more comfortable with ideas and the mental process than you are with experience and feeling. You may have a tendency to place the group before the individual and friends before family and your partner, as well as to sacrifice your own needs for those of a partner.

It's likely that someone close to you brings this conflict into clarity. Perhaps a parent, sibling, or friend urges you to follow your creative dream or to be more selfish in a personal relationship. Listen to this individual.

He or she is here to support your efforts to fulfill your potential as an individual separate from a group. Once you're able to do that, then you're ready to embrace a soul mate relationship that is a bond between genuine equals.

Here are some guidelines for navigating your Leo North Node successfully.

Nurture your creativity. When you learn to do this on a daily basis, out of sheer pleasure and enjoyment, your heart opens up. You begin to realize that it's just fine to seek applause and recognition for what you do and to stand out from the group. It's okay to step onto center stage and announce who you are.

Have fun. It sounds sort of silly to be told you're allowed to have fun, but all too often pleasure and fun are the first things to get shoved aside. You don't have to save the world today. Instead, take time daily to indulge yourself in whatever brings you pleasure and makes you happy.

Ignore peer pressure. The difficulty or ease of this one depends on your age and the type of work you do. A teen may find it as tough a challenge as someone who works in a large bureaucracy where office politics rule the day. If this one seems especially hard for you, then start small. The next time friends want you to do something that you don't feel like doing, just say no.

Create your life. This requires conscious awareness of your internal patterns. The next time you find yourself depending on someone else to make you happy or bring you pleasure, break the pattern by making a conscious decision to create your own happiness. Then get out there and do it!

The Leo North Node is about you as an individual, not you as part of a group or collective; about your creativity rather than everyone else's; about heart, not mind. It urges you to love yourself first so that your heart can open to receiving and giving unconditional love.

Examples: Lewis Carroll, Bon Jovi, Catherine Deneuvre, Arthur Ashe.

♍ IN VIRGO

Your soul is like a Rubik's cube, a three-dimensional puzzle with many intricate parts that somehow must be fit together with utter perfection and attention to detail. To fit all the pieces together, it's necessary to analyze your experiences and to manifest your spiritual beliefs and ideals in a practical way. It's a tall order, because at the heart of your journey lies an inner need for self-perfection.

You're not without tools, however. Your Pisces South Node gives you deep compassion, excellent intuition, healing ability, and easy access to the realm of spirit and imagination. But when you seek this comfort zone out of fear, you may find yourself steeped in victim consciousness or escapism through drugs or alcohol, or you may simply give up because the journey seems so overwhelming.

In relationships, the pitfalls can be twofold. You may fall into a victim/martyr/savior role, which stems from your need to heal others, or you may turn your critical eye on your partner, an offshoot of your quest for perfection. In both instances, you end up feeling trapped and powerless. Here are some simple guidelines to help you avoid any of these roles.

Tackle what you fear. The next time you're unable to make a decision or move forward, take a few moments to explore the fear behind it. Try not to obsess over the fear, to tear it apart and examine each little piece. Simply acknowledge that the fear exists, allow it to move through you, and go on to something else.

Be of service. This is one of the buzz phrases for Virgo. What it really means is sharing your knowledge and skills with other people because you want to and not because you feel obligated to do so. You have tremendous compassion for others, and one way of expressing that compassion is to help others, but without turning yourself into a martyr. In turning your attention away from yourself, your fears evaporate.

Be here now. Ram Dass knew what he was talking about in his book of the same name. By bringing your awareness fully into the present, you realize the present is your point of power. It's the place from which you create your future. When you're here now, your fears don't have a stranglehold over you and you're able to take risks and follow your impulses toward greater growth and fulfillment.

Curb self-criticism. No one is harder on you than you are on yourself, and this tendency usually starts with self-criticism and doubt. I'm not good enough easily becomes I'm not pretty enough or smart enough or deserving enough. The next time you start criticizing yourself, stop immediately, take a deep breath, and repeat: I'm perfect the way I am.

Take charge. Do whatever you have to do to take charge of your life. Set a routine, create goals, develop your creative interests, start an exercise regimen. Then follow through.

Your Virgo North Node is about navigating your daily life. It's left brain to your South Node right brain and allows you to draw on your tremendous imagination to manifest whatever you want and need in your life.

Examples: Michael Crichton, Salvatore Dali, Kobe Bryant.

♎ IN LIBRA

This lifetime is about relationships, specifically about learning how to balance your needs with those of other people. This involves learning cooperation, tact, diplomacy, and mediation, and putting yourself squarely in someone else's shoes.

The comfort zone of your Aries South Node means that you're exceptionally independent and adept at leadership. You tend to be selfish, too. It's not that you're out to hurt anyone else, but just that you believe you must put yourself first in order to survive. Your sense of self is exceptionally well developed, and one of the challenges of this North Node is to learn to value individual differences. Just because someone isn't exactly like you doesn't mean the person isn't worth your time. In fact, it's likely there's someone in your life who already is teaching you this particular lesson—a parent, sibling, another relative, or perhaps even a spouse or partner.

The energy of this nodal axis can be tough to navigate, but here are some simple guidelines to make it easier.

Put others first. If you aren't balking at this one, then congratulations! It means you already have done the hard work. If, however, this attribute seems way too difficult to handle, then try it first in baby steps. Once a month or once a week, for example, put someone else before yourself. It may be something as simple as allowing someone else to go before you in the grocery line. Once you begin to do this on a regular basis, you're advancing along the path of your North Node.

Don't assume you know. Whether it's information or what another person thinks or feels, don't assume that you know. Ask. Communicate. Then make an informed decision. All too often, your Aries South Node compels you to act decisively or impulsively, and that action inadvertently hurts someone else. Part of what you're here to learn is that your actions have consequences.

Learn to compromise. Bite the bullet on this one. Again, if it seems too difficult or challenging, then do it in small ways at first.

Think before you speak. It's called tact. Instead of blurting out the first thing that pops into your head, count to ten first, which is long enough to mull it over. Then add another five beats for good measure!

Your Libra North Node is about others, about relationships in all their magnificent beauty and complexities. Once you master the art of relating to other people, then you'll be able to embrace a soul mate relationship.

Examples: Bill Blass, Tom Brokaw, Frederick Chopin, Ann Margret.

♏ IN SCORPIO

This lifetime is about learning to use personal power in a constructive and positive way. Through intense experiences, you learn to purge your life of what is nonessential or stagnant—relationships, possessions, belief systems, habits—and to embrace partnerships that are mutually supportive.

Your Taurus South Node provides you with plenty of physical energy and stamina, pragmatism, and dogged determination. You aren't afraid of hard work, but you may make some things harder than they need to be. Blame your resistance to change for that. You're an acquisitive person and may even have a particular thing that you collect—art, stamps, or old coins, for example. If you become overly attached to these possessions, then you may attract a situation or circumstances that will teach you the hard way that possessions are just stuff we own.

It's possible that someone in your life mirrors your resistance to change or helps you learn how to embrace change. Or, equally possible, is that you experience situations and events that are profoundly transformative and learn to embrace change because of them. One way or another, you learn the lesson.

Here are guidelines to make your journey easier.

Invite change into your life. Your Taurus South Node may gasp at this suggestion. But it's a necessary step to prevent you from getting stuck in a particular mode of thought, a belief system, or a routine. Once a week or once a month, whatever you feel comfortable with, do something you've never done before. I have one friend, for instance, who hadn't ridden a bike in twenty years. One day she got on a bike and pedaled off into the sunset. It can be something as small as that.

Empower others. You have a knack for empowering others. This doesn't mean you have to sacrifice yourself and your own desires, but that you support other people's creativity, ability to earn money, spiritual values, or whatever is important to them with the same energy that you support your own interests. In a relationship, you can do this by being fully present, by being open and honest in your communications, and by listening to your partner's needs. Once you learn to empower others with the same enthusiasm and dedication that you use to empower yourself, then you're truly in a relationship based on equality. The rewards can be enormous.

Use your intuition. You're exceptionally intuitive. But intuition is like a muscle. The more you use it, the stronger it gets. So use it. Listen to it. You're able to tune in to who people really are—their feelings, motives, or agenda. Once you get used to exercising this muscle, you increase the chance of recognizing your soul mate as soon as you see the person.

Investigate. Whenever you tune in to another person and find something that makes you feel uneasy or anxious, don't pull back. Investigate the feeling. Probe into yourself. Do outside research, if it's called for. Find the source of your feeling. You're a natural detective, and you're looking for the absolute bottom line.

For the Scorpio North Node, a soul mate is what you're looking for and what you will surely find. It can be a sexual, romantic relationship, but it may also be a relationship with a child, a creative partner, a brother or sister, even a friend. Try not to restrict yourself with preconceptions!

Examples: Ansel Adams, Francis Ford Coppola, Judy Collins, Carrie Fisher.

↗ IN SAGITTARIUS

You're here to find your own truth and to do it by using your intuitive ability rather than through an endless collection of facts. In other words, the emphasis this time around is on the right brain, not the left brain; on intuition rather than logic; and on being able to grasp the larger picture.

That said, let's take a look at your comfort zone. Thanks to your Gemini South Node, you love facts, trivia, and information in all shapes and colors, and you rely heavily on logic. You enjoy being with other people, are an excellent networker, have superior writing and speaking skills, and can talk to anyone about virtually anything. But you tend to talk when you should be listening, you often second-guess what people are thinking or feeling, and your energy can be easily scattered. Your logical mind figures it knows all the angles, but it doesn't. You need to find a way to shut down the logic for a while so that your intuition can be heard. It's the only way you're going to find "your truth."

Think of yourself as Diogenes, the mythological figure who carried a lit candle as he made his way through the dark in search of truth. Here are a few simple guidelines to help you navigate this journey through the dark.

Trust yourself. You don't need a dozen opinions before you can make up your mind. You've got it all at your fingertips; listen to that soft, inner voice and then act on its advice.

Be spontaneous. If you feel like flying to Morocco tomorrow, then by all means do it. Allowing yourself spontaneity is part of your Sagittarius North Node package—and so is foreign travel! The more spontaneous you are, the less time you have to gather facts and to think about what you're doing. Spontaneity is your most immediate conduit to your instincts and intuition.

Cultivate patience. Your Gemini South Node reels in horror at this suggestion. But part of what you're learning this time around is that there are no quick answers, no quick fixes. The next time you want your answers yesterday, detach from the situation and ask yourself what the big rush is really about.

It's okay to be wrong sometimes. Part of you craves to be right about everything, all the time. This attitude won't win friends and influence people, and it will make it extremely difficult for you to be involved in any kind of soul mate relationship. This attitude kills curiosity and without curiosity, why bother searching?

The Sagittarius North Node urges you to reach for the unknown. Usually, your spiritual beliefs are an intricate part of the journey. Be aware that one of the risks of this search is self-righteousness.

Examples: Drew Barrymore, George Carlin, Saddam Hussein, Colin Powell.

♑ IN CAPRICORN

This life is about goals—setting them, working to achieve them, and allowing those achievements to bolster your self-esteem. In the process, you have to develop a take-charge attitude about everything else in your life. Bottom line? You have to learn to control your own destiny.

With your Cancer South Node, you have plenty of empathy for other people and instinctively understand how to nurture others. Whether it's a friend with a broken heart, a child in need of sympathy and warmth, or a partner who needs support and understanding, you're there. You even nurture strangers. But when you do this at the expense of your own needs or nurture others without also nurturing yourself, then the comfort zone of your Cancer South Node becomes an obstacle to your achievement. Or, worse, it becomes a prison.

When you fall into your comfort zone in a relationship, you risk smothering your partner, so it's to your advantage to become aware of this pattern in yourself and stop it. What you're striving for, after all, is an equal partnership, not one in which you play Mom. Here are some guidelines to help you navigate your Capricorn North Node.

Release the past. Thanks to your Cancer South Node, you often hug the past against you like a shield, taking refuge in it. Well, eliminate this habit from your life ASAP. Your point of power lies in the present. It's from there you write the script for the rest of your life.

Stay tuned in to your feelings. Stay tuned, by all means, but don't use your emotions to manipulate others. Stay tuned so that you can stay on top of what you feel and understand why you feel what you do. Let negative feelings wash through you rather than obsessing about them. Use positive emotions as a catapult toward change and achievement. You tend to be sentimental, and this emotion often causes you to cling to a relationship or situation long after you should. Don't let your sentimentality stifle your growth.

Listen to your inner voice. You've heard it time and again, the whispering of a small, inner voice that provides guidance, comfort, and information. Think of it as your personal psychic and listen closely when it speaks. Heed its advice.

Express what you feel. Your emotions run deep and sometimes it isn't easy to express them or to share them with a loved one. It may make you feel too vulnerable. But how can there be mutual trust in a partnership if one of you keeps your feelings hidden from the other? If you trust the other person, then be open and honest about your feelings. This suggestion could just as easily read, Say what you mean instead of saying what you think the other person wants to hear. Sometimes you do this because you don't want to deal with confrontation.

Where your Cancer South Node says, "Protect me; take care of me," your Capricorn North Node is telling you it's time to grow up and face the world.

Examples: Indira Gandhi, Sybil Leek, Robert Redford, Oprah Winfrey.

♒ IN AQUARIUS

With an Aquarius North Node, you're here to learn the importance of groups—whether it's a family, a social circle, a community, or the family of humankind. And every group is made up of individuals who view their lives as being just as important as you view your life. You have unique talents and gifts that you must believe in regardless of whether anyone else does. This time around, you're to learn that you can't always be the center of attention.

That last part comes from your Leo South Node, but so does your abundant personal warmth and magnetism. You're adept at manifesting what you want and instinctively know how to win friends and influence people. However, you tend to use excessive emotion to manipulate others and to get what you want, and the longer you do that in this life, the more elusive happiness will seem.

You have a well-developed ego, but ego won't be enough this time around. With this nodal axis, you're required to reach beyond the self and into the larger world to make an impact and a difference through your individual efforts. In other words, the end result isn't about you; it's about the group—the family, the neighborhood, the community, the collective.

Here are some guidelines to help you navigate this North Node more easily.

Don't seek approval. This may be the toughest suggestion for you to follow—and the most important. Whether you're a teenager seeking approval from your peers, a middle-aged parent seeking the approval of your kids, or a man or woman seeking the approval of a partner, it all amounts to the same thing. You're giving your personal power away every time you seek validation from someone else for who you are.

Cultivate creative passions. If you can learn to pour your passionate emotions into a creative outlet, particularly one that brings pleasure or insight or somehow benefits others, then you're on the right track.

Minimize melodrama. It's the actor in you who enjoys those melodramatic moments that put you in the spotlight. The best way to break this habit is by detaching emotionally from whatever set you off. Check out the house placement for your South Node in the next chapter. This will describe the area of your life where you are most likely to be melodramatic.

Perform humanitarian acts. Are you an animal lover? Do you have a soft place in your heart for kids? For the underprivileged? Aquarius is the sign of the humanitarian, and when you begin to live out that part of your nnodal axis, the focus shifts from you to the group.

Where the Leo South Node screams, "Notice me: love me," the Aquarius North Node asks that you seek recognition for the group rather than for yourself.

Examples: David Byrne, Frank Capra, Leonard Cohen, Joan of Arc.

♓ IN PISCES

This lifetime is about discovering the larger spiritual picture that governs your physical life. Your tools include a profound imagination and a finely honed intuition.

With your Virgo South Node, you have a discriminating intellect, are a whiz at attending to details, and seem to feel that everything in your life must be orderly before you can be happy. Orderly is the operative word here. Look to the house placement for your South Node to discover which area of your life the need for order is most likely to manifest itself. You're terrific at creating order from chaos, especially when it's someone else's chaos, but you tend to worry about every little thing. The challenge with this nodal axis is that Virgo sees the trees in the forest—the incredible colors, the texture of the bark, and the lush undergrowth—but can't see the forest or how it fits into a larger landscape.

In terms of relationships, you're looking for the perfect mate, but perfect according to your definition of the word. Because of that, you may overlook potential partners.

Here are some guidelines for moving successfully toward your Pisces North Node.

Develop your spiritual beliefs. Your spiritual path is important in this lifetime, so it's vital that you develop and nurture your spirituality. You benefit from meditation, yoga, tai chi, and similar pursuits. You're happiest when you're earning your living through a line of work where you can combine your imagination and intuition with your spiritual values.

Avoid being critical. When you turn your discriminating intellect on imperfections, you may become overly critical of yourself or others. When this happens, it's the voice of your Virgo South Node speaking. To break the habit, try substituting positive attributes that you see in yourself and others.

Go with the flow. You feel comfortable with routines, where everything is defined and categorized, known and understood. But this actually stifles the creative voice of your imagination. Try, instead, to go with the flow, even when it disrupts your routine and threatens to bring you face to face with the unknown. In the process, you'll discover that your own pace slows down and that you're able to accomplish more than you would have if you had resisted the flow.

Trust the universe. This suggestion is challenging. Whenever you come up against a situation or relationship that you don't understand, your

Virgo South Node instantly starts gathering details, trying to connect the dots and make sense of what's going on. A better use of your time and energy is simply to release your concerns and trust in a high power.

While your Virgo South Node slaps its ruler on your desktop and demands that you do your duty, pay attention to details, and perfect, perfect, your Pisces North Node whispers, "Relax, it's going to be come out okay in the end."

Examples: Naomi Campbell, Matt Damon, Isadora Duncan, Mark Hamill.

FAMILIES, FRIENDS, AND NORTH NODES

An excellent way to grasp the importance and meaning of the North Node in your life is to look up the signs of the North Nodes for members of your family or for friends you have known for many years. Because these are the people you often know the best and for the longest time, you'll know whether the descriptions in this chapter fit your family members and close friends.

My astrologer friend, Renie, studied my daughter's chart when she was about three days old. One of her first observations concerned Megan's Nodes. "She's going to be dramatic and may pursue acting, dance, or some facet of entertainment. Encourage that creative expression. Through it, she'll learn how to cooperate with people in a group situation. She'll learn that the world doesn't revolve around her."

Megan has her South Node in Leo and her North Node in Aquarius. And she is dramatic. Her emotions are right at the surface. She's quick to express herself, has deep empathy, and attends a public high school that emphasizes acting for television and motion pictures. And through her acting, she's learning the path of her North Node in Aquarius—that no actor executes his or her craft in a vacuum.

Sometimes you find similar patterns within families. Megan, her grandmother, her aunt, and one of her cousins all share the Aquarius/Leo nnodal axis. By house, Megan and her dad share a twelfth house North Node. And because astrology is about patterns, repetitive patterns like this are significant. It's almost as if there are karmic families within our blood families that are working on the same issues.

Take a few moments to look up your family's North Node signs.

THE NODES IN THE HOUSES

H ouses: we build them, live in them, refurbish them, buy and sell them. The houses have rooms and each room has a function. The houses in a birth chart are more like the rooms in our own homes, with each one symbolic of a particular area of life—finances, for example, or career or romance. The sign that was rising when you were born, known as the ascendant, or rising, sign, determines the layout of the houses in your birth chart.

If the sign of Libra was rising when you were born, then Libra is considered to be the cusp of your first house. That means that if your Sun or one of your Nodes is in Libra, it would fall in your first house. With a Libra rising, Scorpio would be on the cusp of your second house, Sagittarius on the cusp of your third, and so on around the horoscope until you end up with Virgo on the cusp of your twelfth house.

The only way to have an accurate Ascendant for your birth horoscope is to have your chart drawn up by an astrologer or a computer. If you have access to the Internet, go to **www.janspiller.com**, click on free personal charts, then click on free natal birth chart, enter your birth data, verify the

TABLE 4: YOUR RISING SIGN

Rising Sign → / Sun Sign ↓	♈	♉	♊	♋	♌
♈ Aries	5 A.M.	7 A.M.	9 A.M.	11 A.M.	1 P.M.
♉ Taurus	3 A.M.	5 A.M.	7 A.M.	9 A.M.	11 A.M.
♊ Gemini	1 A.M.	3 A.M.	5 A.M.	7 A.M.	9 A.M.
♋ Cancer	11 P.M.	1 A.M.	3 A.M.	5 A.M.	7 A.M.
♌ Leo	9 P.M.	11 P.M.	1 A.M.	3 A.M.	5 A.M.
♍ Virgo	7 P.M.	9 P.M.	11 P.M.	1 A.M.	3 A.M.
♎ Libra	5 P.M.	7 P.M.	9 P.M.	11 P.M.	1 A.M.
♏ Scorpio	3 P.M.	5 P.M.	7 P.M.	9 P.M.	11 P.M.
♐ Sagittarius	1 P.M.	3 P.M.	5 P.M.	7 P.M.	9 P.M.
♑ Capricorn	11 A.M.	1 P.M.	3 P.M.	5 P.M.	7 P.M.
♒ Aquarius	9 A.M.	11 A.M.	1 P.M.	3 P.M.	5 P.M.
♓ Pisces	7 A.M.	9 A.M.	11 A.M.	1 P.M.	3 P.M.

data, and sit back. The chart that comes up on your screen is your natal blueprint and includes the house placement and sign of your North Node (☊). The South Node isn't shown, but it falls in the house and sign directly opposite. So if your North Node is in Aquarius in the twelfth house, your South Node will be in Leo in the sixth house.

If you don't have access to a computer—or to a library where you can use the Internet—then use Table 4 to estimate your rising sign.

Once you've estimated your rising sign, now use one of the blank horoscopes in the back of the book and place your rising sign on the left-hand side of the horizontal line between houses one and twelve. Moving counterclockwise around the horoscope circle, put the next sign on the line between houses one and two, and so on around until you reach the point where you started. So, back to our earlier example, if Libra is your rising sign, then Scorpio goes on the cusp of the second house (the line between houses one and two), Sagittarius on the cusp of the third house, Capricorn on the cusp of the fourth, and on around the chart.

♍	♎	♏	♐	♑	♒	♓
3 P.M.	5 P.M.	7 P.M.	9 P.M.	11 P.M.	1 A.M.	3 A.M.
1 P.M.	3 P.M.	5 P.M.	7 P.M.	9 P.M.	11 P.M.	1 A.M.
11 A.M.	1 P.M.	3 P.M.	5 P.M.	7 P.M.	9 P.M.	11 P.M.
9 A.M.	11 A.M.	1 P.M.	3 P.M.	5 P.M.	7 P.M.	9 P.M.
7 A.M.	9 A.M.	11 A.M.	1 P.M.	3 P.M.	5 P.M.	7 P.M.
5 A.M.	7 A.M.	9 A.M.	11 A.M.	1 P.M.	3 P.M.	5 P.M.
3 A.M.	5 A.M.	7 A.M.	9 A.M.	11 A.M.	1 P.M.	3 P.M.
1 A.M.	3 A.M.	5 A.M.	7 A.M.	9 A.M.	11 A.M.	1 P.M.
11 P.M.	1 A.M.	3 A.M.	5 A.M.	7 A.M.	9 A.M.	11 A.M.
9 P.M.	11 P.M.	1 A.M.	3 A.M.	5 A.M.	7 A.M.	9 A.M.
7 P.M.	9 P.M.	11 P.M.	1 A.M.	3 A.M.	5 A.M.	7 A.M.
5 P.M.	7 P.M.	9 P.M.	11 P.M.	1 A.M.	3 A.M.	5 A.M.

Next, place your Nodes in their appropriate houses. If your North Node is in Scorpio, then your South Node is in Taurus. The North Node would go in your second house and the South Node in your eighth.

With some horoscopes, a sign is intercepted or contained within a particular house. If Scorpio is rising, and Sagittarius appears on the cusp of the second house—but it also appears on the cusp of the third. Then look directly across the chart to houses eight and nine; Gemini appears on the cusp of both of these houses. This means two signs will be intercepted or contained with other houses. Look at house six; Pisces is on the cusp of that house (29♓36), so Aries should be on the cusp of the seventh. But Aries falls within the sixth house (♈), and Taurus is on the cusp of the seventh house (00♉50). Directly across from the sixth house, Libra (♎) falls within the twelfth house. This is due to the size of the houses and means that the energy of these two signs must be taken into account when talking about the activities of the sixth and twelfth houses.

If you're estimating your chart, interceptions won't appear because you're using just signs, not degrees, for the cusps of the houses. So if you're using an estimated chart, keep this in mind as you read through interpretations.

Now you've got a birth chart in front of you. But suppose you want your partner's chart, too? Astrologer and author Jan Spiller's site allows you only one free chart, so unless you join for $3.95 a month, which allows you unlimited charts, you should go to **www.astro.com**, click on free charts, and enter your partner's birth data. The chart that comes up won't show your partner's Nodes, but you can use the ephemeris in this book to find out the sign for the North Node and place it in the appropriate house. Once again, the South Node will fall in the opposite sign and house.

Whew. Now you're ready to find out what it all means.

THE HOUSES

This section describes the sign that was rising when you were born— your Ascendant (**AS**).

ASCENDENT AND FIRST HOUSE: Who You Are

The Ascendant, or rising, sign of a chart is considered one of four critical angles in a horoscope. It symbolizes your public face and the way others perceive you. Its sign rules your first house, which symbolizes your overall personality. Folded into the first house is information about your early childhood, your general health, and your modes of self-expression.

North Node first house, South Node seventh house: Your path is to consciously develop your talents and abilities independently of a partner. Until you're able to do that, you may attract partners through whom you seek to sculpt your identity. The closer the North Node is to the Ascendant, the stronger the need to excel as an individual rather than as half of a whole in a relationship. Your tendency is to let other people make decisions for you, such as a parent, a partner, or someone in authority. But you need to be decisive, aggressive, and independent, and realize you're the scriptwriter of your own life.

Take a look at this lineup: Writer and TV commentator Bill Moyers and John Lennon (North Node on the Ascendant), writer and Nobel prize winner Pearl Buck, writer Shirley Jackson, writer Sylvia Plath, writer F. Scott Fitzgerald.

Fitzgerald's nodal axis is especially interesting in light of his relationship with his wife, Zelda. He had a North Node in Aquarius in the first house and a Leo South Node in the seventh house. He constantly sought approval and recognition for his talents and abilities (South Node Leo) but was able to develop his talents as a writer to such an extreme degree that he pretty much defined the Roaring Twenties. However, he did this at the expense of his health and his wife and partner, Zelda, who felt that he stole elements of their life together to create his fiction. Zelda went nuts and Fitzgerald subsequently felt that he prostituted his talent to pay for her medical bills.

SECOND HOUSE: Your Personal Values

This house describes your personal values, finances, material resources, assets and expenditures, and attitude toward money. It's also about how you earn and spend money, your attitude toward material possessions, and your earning power. Themes such as self-worth are also included in this house.

North Node second house, South Node eighth house: Your path is to define your values separate from your family, spouse, friends, or any other group to which you belong. Your earning potential is important to you and may be tied up somehow with your identity. It's possible that you're a workaholic. You're willing to share your resources and knowledge, which are considerable, but may not be quite so generous when it comes to sharing your hard-earned money.

Walt Disney, for example, was born into poverty and was abused by his father as a child. He went to work at the age of ten, delivering news-papers, and worked incessantly until his death at age sixty-five. He made the first feature-length animation film (*Fantasia*) and created Disneyland and Disney Studios, an empire that is even vaster today. He collected cuckoo clocks, was obsessed with trains, and apparently wasn't the greatest guy to work for. But he had a vision and worked relentlessly to make it happen.

Carl Jung is an excellent example of how this nodal axis works. His Aries North Node in the second house emphasizes the pioneering spirit that marked his life and work. His Libra South Node in the eighth house indicated a deep interest in the hidden side of life—dreams, the paranormal, astrology, and mythology.

In an attempt to define himself, he went where others had not, developing theories on synchronicity, archetypes, the collective unconscious, and the anima and animus. His ideas ran contrary to the consensus beliefs of his time and eventually spelled the end of his friendship with Freud. He was married to his wife, Emma, for fifty-five years, but he had numerous affairs throughout his life, including a long-term relationship with his mistress, Toni Wolff.

THIRD HOUSE: Communication

This house represents your conscious mind and the daily activities in your life. It describes how you communicate and learn; your mental attitudes; your experiences with siblings, relatives, and neighbors; and your place in the community or neighborhood in which you live. Travel is also included here, but as trips to the next town rather than a journey to the South Pacific.

North Node in the third house, South Node in the ninth house: To evolve and grow, it's necessary to expand your belief system. Education, learning, books, and communication of all types are instrumental in the expansion of your beliefs. You gain information through writing and communicating your knowledge. Your siblings or your neighborhood may play into this process, and you strive to develop your relationships with these people. Mutual communication is vital to the success of any of your intimate partnerships. You may have unusual intellectual abilities and a firm grasp of foreign cultures, philosophies, and belief systems.

Deepak Chopra has this nodal axis. Thanks to his Sagittarius South Node in the ninth house, be brings his East Indian heritage to the twenty-plus books he has written on holistic health. His books incorporate

Ayurvedic medicine, quantum physics, and the role of consciousness in the practice and maintenance of health.

Tina Turner's North Node in Libra in the third house certainly can be seen in her communication through music. The Libra part of the equation (think relationships here) is obvious in her long-term partnership with Ike Turner. She and Ike were married for twenty-two years, but for most of those years the relationship was an abusive one. Tina got out in 1978, went into hiding, and lived on food stamps. Finally, in the early 1980s, she was on the rise again, and in 1984, her album, "Private Dancer," hit the big time. It ultimately sold more than 10 million copies worldwide. By then, she was living with a younger man, had several homes in Europe, and was on top once again.

In addition to music, she has written a book, *I, Tina,* starred in the *Mad Max* films, and done TV commercials. In short, she certainly has lived out that Libra North Node.

FOURTH HOUSE: Your Home and Roots

The fourth house is the second critical angle of the horoscope. This house symbolizes your home—the one you had growing up and the one you create for yourself as an adult. It symbolizes your experience with one of your parents, your early childhood and usually the last twenty years or so of your life, your roots, and real estate. This house is the cellar of the chart, with all the attendant shadows and nooks and crannies we associate with cellars. That's probably why the fourth house is also associated with the collective unconscious.

North Node in the fourth house, South Node in the tenth house: This path is about learning the value of family and ancestry and balancing it against the demands of your career and the outer world. You may not be crazy about putting your family ahead of your career, but that's the hand you chose this time around. One of your parents, often the mother, plays a role in this process, and you're close to her. In this nodal position, your home as an adult and your role as a parent come into play. The closer the Node is to the cusp of the fourth house, the stronger its influence.

Lucille Ball is a fascinating example of this nodal axis. By focusing on home and family in the *I Love Lucy Show,* she and her husband, Desi Arnaz, mined a vein of gold that captured 40 million viewers, won her the reputation as one of the great female comedians, and made her a multi-millionaire. Even her kids became part of the show. True to the Taurus North Node, she was a shrewd businesswoman with tremendous clout. After she and Arnaz divorced, she bought out his share in Desilu Studio and ran it for seven years. She eventually sold it to Gulf and Western for a reported $17 million.

Other luminaries with this nodal axis include Henry Ford, Kevin Costner, and George Lucas.

FIFTH HOUSE: Creativity, Children, and Romance

This is the house where we enjoy ourselves! Think pleasure, romance, gambling, speculation, sex for fun, creativity, and children, particularly the first-born. Any or all of these areas can be highlighted when the North Node falls here. At various times in your life, one aspect may be the focus of your activities, but then you move on and another aspect becomes the focus.

North Node in the fifth house, South Node in the eleventh house: Your comfort zone lies within groups and group activities. But this time around, you're meant to develop your own creative voice. It will be the deepest source of your spiritual growth and, in some way, will define who you are. At some point in your life, it will be necessary for you to break away from group associations so that you're free enough of peer pressure to explore your creativity. Children are important to you and may contribute to your creativity in some vital way. Your love affairs and romances often have past-life connections that you feel, even if you don't always understand that feeling.

The artist Paul Cézanne had this nodal axis, with a Capricorn North Node in the fifth house. True to the creative voice of this placement, Cézanne's entire life was devoted to the cultivation of his creative abilities. A boyhood friendship with Emile Zola was instrumental in Cézanne's moving to Paris against the wishes of his father, who wanted Cézanne to enter the field of law. Even though Cézanne became acquainted with other artists of his era—Monet and Renoir, for example—and eventually attracted the attention of other Impressionists, he maintained a solitary life. He eventually married a woman eleven years younger and had a son with her, but they spent much of their married lives apart. Today, Cézanne is considered the spiritual father of Impressionism.

Galileo also had this nodal axis. The "group" that he had to break away from was the Roman Catholic Church, which took exception to his theory that the Sun—rather than the Earth—was the center of the solar system. When he was sixty-nine years old, he was charged with heresy and was forced to repudiate his theories. The church banned his books for nearly 200 years after his death.

SIXTH HOUSE: Daily Work

This house could also be called "your daily bread." It's about your daily work routine, your daily health, and your daily responsibilities. It describes the tasks you perform on the job, your relationships with employees and employers, and anything you do in a service capacity—that is, a service to others without compensation.

North Node in the sixth house, South Node in the twelfth: In a sense, your daily work becomes your life and your spiritual path. With the North Node in the sixth house, your general health is stronger and spontaneous remissions are possible. It's necessary to develop a deeper awareness about your physical health and its connection to your spiritual beliefs and your emotions. Once you do, this may become part of your spiritual path. You benefit from meditation and alternative healing methods.

With this nodal axis, it isn't surprising to find people involved in the health field—Sigmund Freud, for example, and Alois Alzheimer, the German physician who investigated the pathology of senility and after whom Alzheimer's disease is named. Freud, like Jung, had a North Node in Aries, the sign of the pioneer. Alzheimer's North Node in Scorpio is the sign of the researcher who seeks the absolute bottom line.

Erma Bombeck, with a North Node in Cancer, the sign of the home, began her career by writing a humorous column about home life in suburbia. Within a year, it was syndicated across the country. She certainly achieved the potential of the North Node in the sixth house.

SEVENTH HOUSE: Partnership

Business and romantic partnerships, marriage, and contracts all go here. It describes the types of partners you are likely to attract, what you're looking for in an intimate relationship, and your ability to be involved in intimate relationships. The cusp of this house is the third critical angle of a horoscope.

North Node in the seventh house, South Node in the first house: With this nodal axis, you evolve spiritually through marriage and other partnerships. In fact, one-on-one partnerships are extremely important to you. It may be that you need to learn to compromise or to put someone else's concerns before your own. Or maybe your path involves being more aware of public sentiment and opinion. With the North Node in the seventh house, your focus for this lifetime is others rather than yourself. Once you learn this, you will realize that what you accomplish with a partner is greater than anything you can accomplish alone.

Many people with this North Node position have multiple marriages, perhaps because intimacy is part of what they're learning. William Peter Blatty, for example, author of *The Exorcist*, has been married four times and so has music legend Willie Nelson. Mystery writer Sue Grafton is on her third marriage.

But the partnership part of the equation sometimes translates as an intimate relationship with "the public." Michael J. Fox has been married to the same woman since 1988. But he is wildly popular as a TV and movie star and, in 1998, when he went public with the fact that he had been diagnosed with Parkinson's disease seven years earlier, it made an impact. He is now an advocate of stem cell research.

EIGHTH HOUSE: Transformation

Think Woody Allen with this house: sex, death, and taxes. But the eighth house also encompasses shared resources, insurance, the affairs of the dead, estates, reincarnation, sexuality, life after death, and the darker or hidden side of life. It's about profound transformation and the experiences that bring about that transformation.

North Node in the eighth house, South Node in the second house: Your path is to share your resources with others. This includes all sorts of resources—financial, emotional, spiritual, and social, as well as anything else that might be considered a resource. The hidden part of life will hold an undeniable attraction for you. You enjoy mystery, intrigue, the paranormal, and anything mystical, offbeat, or downright bizarre.

This nodal axis can be one of extremes, particularly in people who are fascinated by the sexual facet of the North Node in the eighth house. The Marquis de Sade, a man whose name seems to be synonymous with sadism, is one of the most blatant examples. Screenwriter David Lynch expresses the steamy, weird side of the eighth house Node in movies such as *Blue Velvet* and *Wild at Heart.* His occult interests came through in *Dune.*

Then there's Cat Stevens, an excellent example of the spiritual side of this nodal placement. The multitalented Stevens was a musician, songwriter, pianist, guitarist, and a major voice in the '60s. Then, in 1979, after a near-drowning experience, he converted to the Muslim religion, changed his name, and dropped off the musical radar.

NINTH HOUSE: Your Worldview

Think of this house as your soul's hard drive. Your experiences with the larger world go here—your higher education, spiritual and religious beliefs, philosophy, interest in other cultures and foreign-born people, travel to foreign countries, the law, politics, and even astrology. Your interests are vast and will lead you in unexpected directions. At some point, your ability to gather information will have to become more focused so that you can synthesize all your experiences into a worldview that feels right for you. And that's what this house is about in the end: your worldview. It's through this house that you expand your understanding of society and the world.

North Node in the ninth house, South Node in the third house: Your path in this lifetime is to reach beyond the country and beliefs that you consider home and embrace all that is alien to you so that you can broaden your outlook. You'll have ample opportunities to do this through education, travel, a variety of spiritual experiences, and interaction generally with the larger world in which you live. Let's take a look at how this happens in real life.

J.R.R. Tolkien had his North Node here. He gave us a world complete with hobbits that have their own culture, challenges, and quests. When you read the *Lord of the Rings* trilogy (or watch the movies), you become fully immersed in this fictional world. Everything springs to life—the size and funny shapes of the hobbit houses, the way the hobbits look with their big feet and funny ears —and you have a very real feeling for the characters Bilbo, Frodo, and the great Gandalf. Tolkien certainly lived out the energy of his North Node through writing.

Bill Clinton also has his North Node here and is living out its energy through politics. Even though he doesn't hold a public office now, he is just as active on the Democratic scene, speaking at rallies and raising campaign money. He even has a book deal, another ninth house pursuit.

Bob Dylan has been at the forefront of music for decades. The popularity of his music isn't limited to the U.S.—he's just as popular overseas, another manifestation of North Node energy.

TENTH HOUSE: Profession and Career

You're a fireman, policeman, teacher, writer, Indian chief, or CEO: This house represents how others see you and the labels they give you. It's called the house of profession and career. Where the fourth house is the private you, the tenth house is the public you. The cusp of this house is the fourth critical angle of a horoscope.

North Node in the tenth house, South Node in the third house: Part of your path this time around is to reach into the public world and strive to achieve in whatever field you choose. Your early childhood and family are instrumental in shaping the person you become and the ways in which you strive to attain your goals. You may always feel torn between your obligations to your family and those to your career, but this tension is the heart of your springboard to success.

Look at the lineup here: Stephen King, Michael Caine, Meryl Streep, radio talk show host Art Bell, Agatha Christie, Nat King Cole, Jamie Lee Curtis, and novelist John Irving. Take King. He's an extremely private man, yet his name is synonymous with books that dig into our deepest fears. His father abandoned the family when King was quite young, and he lived much of his childhood in poverty. His books have sold millions of copies worldwide, but he recently received the literary recognition he felt eluded him and which he certainly deserved: a National Book Award for lifetime achievement.

Michael Caine grew up in the slums of post-war London, where his father worked in a fish market and his mother was a cleaning woman. He was a dropout at the age of sixteen, and yet he has starred in more than seventy films and won several Oscars—the most recent in 2000 for his supporting role in *Cider House Rules*.

If you look at the lives of people with a North Node in the tenth house, the delicate balance between family obligations and career is usually evident. With this position, fame and renown is certainly possible—but so is infamy. Ted Bundy also had his North Node in the tenth house.

ELEVENTH HOUSE: Ideals and Dreams

This house used to be somewhat vague to me, a kind of way station in the zodiac, where I was forced to hesitate, reassess, and reevaluate what I thought it meant. Part of it was that I don't have any planets in this house and neither does my husband or daughter. But my mother had four planets in the eleventh and my sister has two. Once I began to study their charts and, subsequently, the charts of friends, clients, and public figures, I finally got it.

The eleventh house is about support groups. I don't mean AA—although that's one possibility—but bridge groups, theater groups, writers' groups, groups with people who share our interests, dreams, and passions and whose support helps us realize our deepest dreams. And through the realization of our most personal dreams, we somehow touch the lives of other people—society, the public, humanity.

North Node in the eleventh house, South Node in the fifth house: Your path in this life is to develop an awareness of the power of groups in achieving individual dreams and in bringing about change in the world. Your friends and group associations are important to you and, in some way, support your hopes and ideals. You may sometimes feel as if you don't have time for your personal creativity, but the fact is that you can reach your personal creative goals much more quickly with a little help from your friends.

Your comfort zone lies in romance and children. You enjoy the whole package of romance and probably fall in love easily, but you quickly find yourself immersed in emotional dramas. Your children may be a cause for concern.

Steven Spielberg, Charles Lindberg, Toni Morrison, Harrison Ford, and Frank Capra all have their North Node in the eleventh house. The group nature of the eleventh house often translates into a public appeal through the creative work done in the fifth house. Yet, despite the public appeal that people with this node placement often have, there's a tendency toward great personal privacy. Look at Harrison Ford, famous for the *Star Wars* trilogies and *Indiana Jones* movies, one of the hottest male stars around. Yet he maintains an almost obsessive privacy about his personal life.

TWELFTH HOUSE: Personal Unconscious

In traditional astrology, the twelfth house sounds like my version of hell: incarceration, confinement, karma, and secret enemies. But when you take an in-depth look at the twelfth house, the bottom line is that it's about the power we have disowned or repressed over the course of our present lives and issues that we have brought in from previous lives. It represents our personal unconscious and everything that is hidden. In contemporary Western society, the "hidden" aspect of the twelfth house is found in nursing homes, hospitals, jails, and prisons, places where society's "undesirables" are kept.

North Node in the twelfth house, South Node in the sixth house: Your path is one of inner exploration, where you are required to dive into the sea of your own unconscious and make sense of it. A tall order, perhaps, but one way to make this journey much easier is to make sure that your daily work complements and enhances your deepest needs and desires.

The sign of the North Node will tell you a great deal about how you should do this. If, for instance, your North Node is in Aquarius, then it's essential that you learn to detach from your emotions by understanding what makes you feel you have to be on center stage all the time or why you seek the approval of others.

Joseph Campbell lived out his twelfth house nodal placement by delving into mythology, which certainly falls into the realm of this house. By the time he died at the age of eighty-three, he was one of the world's leading authorities on mythology, the psyche, and symbolism.

The
COMBINATIONS

"Life is meant to be a mystery…"

— Caroline Myss,
author and medical intuitive

The material in part two has several different levels of information that are derived from the angles between your and your partner's Sun signs and between your respective Sun signs and North Nodes. Because you are separate individuals with separate horoscopes, the information concerning Sun signs and Nodes probably won't be the same for both of you.

Before we work through a real life example, remove two of the blank wheels in the back of the book. At the top, label one of them "Pauline" and label the other one "Steve." These individuals both have their natal charts, so this example is a little different and more accurate than what you'll get if you don't have your and your partner's natal chart. But we'll get to that in a minute.

The houses on the blank wheels are already numbered for you. On Pauline's wheel, write "Sagittarius" at the line that separates houses twelve and one. This is her Ascendant, or rising, sign. Now continue counter-clockwise around the chart, filling in each subsequent sign, with Capricorn on the cusp of her second house, Aquarius on the cusp of the third, Pisces on the cusp of the fourth, and so on around the wheel until you end up with Scorpio on the cusp of the twelfth house.

Pauline is a Pisces with a North Node in Sagittarius. Her Pisces Sun falls in the fourth house. Jot this information—☉♓—(Sun in Pisces) in her fourth house. She has a North Node in Sagittarius—☊♐—in her first house. Jot this in the first house.

Now bring out the wheel labeled Steve. He has Libra rising, so begin your labeling of the houses with Libra, then Scorpio on the cusp of the second house, Sagittarius on the cusp of the third, and on around the chart. You'll end up with Virgo on the cusp of the twelfth house. Steve is a Capricorn with a North Node in Leo. His Capricorn Sun—☉♑—falls in his fourth house. Jot the symbols in his fourth house. His Leo North Node—☊♌—falls in his eleventh house. Jot the symbols in the eleventh house on his chart.

We now have two independent pictures. Before Pauline and Steve dive into part two, they should read about their respective Sun signs and North Nodes, as well as the house placement descriptions for their natal Suns and North Nodes. Once they've done that, they can begin to piece together a larger picture of their relationship.

Let's do Pauline's chart first. Place Steve's Capricorn Sun in her second house. You may want to place it just outside the second house, in the margin, to distinguish it from her planets. Now place his North Node in Leo just outside her ninth house. You immediately have a visual picture of their relationship. First, look at the placement of their respective Sun signs—they're separated by two signs (always count the house in which the Sun is positioned as the first sign). This means their respective Sun signs fall under the heading of "Best Friends, Two Signs Apart" (chapter 7), and that she should read the "Capricorn/Pisces Couple" entry. It describes how they relate to each other in their relationship. Regardless of what else Pauline and Steve may be to each other, they are genuinely best friends.

Take a look at Pauline's chart again. Notice that Steve's North Node falls in her ninth house. That means that her natal Sun in the fourth house and his North Node are separated by five signs and are described in chapter 10, "Magician, Five Signs Apart." She should skip to the middle of the chapter and read only the appropriate section under the heading "Sun/North Node Connections—Fourth House/Ninth House Couple." This describes their karmic path as a couple.

So by reading about their Sun sign combinations in "Best Friends" and their Sun/North Node connections in "Magician," Pauline comes away with deeper insight into her relationship with Steve. However, it would be to her advantage to read the appropriate sections in part one about Steve's Sun sign, the sign of his North Node, and the house place-ments—according to his natal chart—for the Sun and the Node.

What about Steve? On his wheel, you're now going to place Pauline's Sun sign and North Node according to where they fall in his chart. Her Pisces Sun falls in Steve's sixth house; insert ☉♓ in the outer rim of his sixth house, so that we know it's her Sun. Her North Node in Sagittarius—☊♐—falls in his third house, so place those symbols in the outer rim of Steve's third house.

Their Sun signs, of course, still fall two signs apart, so he would read the "Capricorn/Pisces Couple" section in chapter 7. But the Sun/North Node connections for Steve are vastly different; his Capricorn Sun is separated from her Sagittarius North Node by just one sign, which is found in "Equals, One Sign Apart" (chapter 6). He should skip the descriptions of the Sun combinations in this chapter, page directly to the Sun/North Node descriptions, and read the entry under "Third House/Fourth House Couple."

For those who don't have natal charts, follow the same process as the one for Pauline and Steve, but you and your partner should put your respective Sun signs on the Ascendant of blank wheels. In other words, if you have a Gemini Sun, put that sign on the Ascendant, then move counterclockwise around the wheel, filling in each subsequent sign. Cancer would be on the cusp of the second, Leo on the cusp of the third, and on around the wheel. Your partner would do the same thing with his or her wheel.

For each of you, your Sun sign would be placed in the first house (because we've put your Sun sign on the Ascendant) and your North Node would be placed in the appropriate house. This technique will work fine for the Sun sign combination descriptions, but it may not be as accurate in terms of the Sun/North Node connections.

If you have your birth data but for some reason can't download your natal chart from one of the sites provided earlier in the book, drop me an e-mail at **www.booktalk.com/tjmacgregor** and I'll e-mail you a chart.

LOVERS

SAME SIGN

Think back for a moment about your life. If you can remember the Sun signs of people you've been involved with, which signs have you gotten along with best? Have you ever been involved with someone who has the same Sun sign that you do? If you've never been romantically involved with a person who shares your Sun sign, then look around at your other relationships—within your immediate family, your relatives and closest friends, even your business partnerships—for people who were born under your Sun sign. How did those relationships differ from others?

Several months ago, a freelance reporter for a South Florida newspaper interviewed me. During our conversation, I began to feel that she might be a Gemini and, of course, had to ask. It turned out that not only is she a Gemini, but we also share the same birthdate and year. We are what astrologers call astral twins. It's eerie to even talk to an astral twin. Your mindset, your attitudes, your passions and challenges are hauntingly familiar. The details differ, but many of the broad strokes are the same.

In fact, anyone whose Sun sign is the same as yours and who is born within a couple of days of your birthdate will feel like family to you. My sister, a Capricorn, recently dated a man who was born within a week of her birthdate, and in the same year. When I did their respective charts, I loved what I saw in terms of compatibility and soul mate connections. There were other things I saw in his chart that bothered me, mostly having to do with his early childhood, but I figured those details could be overcome because of the strength in synergy in their charts. Even my sister said that when she was with this man, it was as if they had known each other for years. They enjoyed the same things, often completed each other's sentences. You know the kind of relationship I mean. It feels so right that you wonder how you'll get through the night if the relationship doesn't work out.

I wish I could say that my sister married this guy and lived happily ever after. But he had emotional baggage and what we now call "issues" that ended the relationship after just four months. So was the astrology wrong? Not at all. Free will is always the decisive factor. Just because you and a partner share conjunctions between your Sun signs, between your Nodes, or between your Nodes and your Sun signs, doesn't guarantee that the relationship will endure until death. But it does indicate that the psychological tone of the relationship is that of lovers who share a wonderful closeness.

In the event you share Sun or nodal conjunctions with a parent, child, friend, or someone else in your life who isn't a romantic partner, the same psychological tone holds true. You'll share a deep closeness and probably have been together in past lives.

One of my friends, a Leo, has a Leo son with whom she enjoys a wonderfully close relationship. She is supportive of his decisions, dreams, and aspirations—and vice versa. She knows they have been together many times in previous lives and has had several repeating dreams that are, she says, more like memories, that seem to support this. However, for the purpose of this book, the descriptions in this and other chapters are specifically geared toward romantic partners.

Sun Sign Combinations

This section describes how you and your partner relate to each other.

♈ ♈

ARIES COUPLE

This combination is passionate and volatile. You're both independent, impulsive, and impatient people who often seem to be living your lives jammed in fast forward. If you can slow down enough to agree on what you want to do right now, then there's hope that you can figure out where the relationship is headed tomorrow or a month from now!

Whether you're cooking, making love, or driving a car, both of you have your own ideas about how things should be done. There may be squabbles related to these kinds of issues, but sooner or later one of you learns to give in some of the time to the other or you both learn the art of—gasp!—cooperation.

Fortunately, you share a fearlessness that propels you on one adventure after another and as long as one can keep up with the other, things are great. But when your desires diverge—one of you wants to hang out at home, for instance, and the other wants to hike the Appalachian Trail—then there's trouble. In an ideal world, you would go your separate ways for the day with no hard feelings. After all, you're two very independent people. But given the fiery emotions both of you have, a divergence of wills may lead to problems until you both understand that you've come together in this life to support and learn from each other.

At some level, you're both thrill seekers and enjoy excitement regardless of how it's wrapped. When you come up against obstacles in life, you probably respond the same way—you ram the obstacle again and again until it finally crumbles. Given the ardent, passionate nature of most Aries individuals, your sexual relationship won't ever be boring, but you both tend to be jealous or suspicious when you feel your partner may not be faithful to you.

$$\bigcup \bigcup$$

TAURUS COUPLE

This relationship is extremely sensual, and the sensuality finds expression in many ways—lovemaking, the foods you enjoy, your mutual respect for nature, and perhaps even in the care that you give to your physical bodies. If you share an interest in things that go bump in the night, mysticism, spirituality, or deeper unknowns, then so much the better. The spiritual glue will hold you together when you're both too stubborn to admit you're wrong.

Taurus, a fixed sign represented by the bull, is the most stubborn in the zodiac. Bring two of them together in a romantic partnership and it could redefine the word stubborn. That said, part of the reason you've come together is that each of you may have to learn when to stick to your respective opinions or beliefs and when to admit that you're not always right. What better place to learn this than in a romantic partnership, where the one place you get along almost all the time is in bed?

Your mutual physical attraction for each other compensates for those moments when you feel like strangling your partner because he or she is "so stubborn."

Your relationship is apt to be quite private, because it's something you both value. As a couple, you may prefer to hang out at home on Saturday night and whip up some delectable gourmet dish and enjoy it with a bottle of great wine. Or you may want to take in a concert. One of your common interests should be a love of music and one or both of you may have musical talent. Equally possible is a weekend in the woods or at the beach or even strolling through the museums of a city neither of you has ever visited. Some Taureans are rugged outdoors people; others are creatures of extreme comfort. If you are one type and your partner is the other, there could be some friction. But it's nothing insurmountable.

$$\mathrm{II}\ \mathrm{II}$$

GEMINI COUPLE

Every pairing has its quirks, and this one certainly has more than its share. As one of the two signs represented by two of something (the twins), there are actually four of you to contend with in this relationship—two of each of you. The trick to making a success of this crowded state of affairs is to understand your own duality first. On a given day, which twin directs your life? The optimist or the pessimist? The lion or the lamb? The geek or the comic? Right brain or left brain? Once you understand your duality, it's easier to understand and live with your partner's duality.

As an air sign, Gemini is a communicator and extremely comfortable in the world of ideas. When you get two Geminis together, there's usually lots of talking, but there may not be much listening. You and your partner are so intent on saying your piece that you sometimes forget to really listen to each other. Because you're both mutable signs, you may have trouble making up your minds as a couple or, for that matter, committing to each other in any kind of formal way.

For both of you, though, communication is the key to your heart, and if you and your partner have a deep rapport, then the rest will come fairly easily. In fact, if you and your partner don't connect mentally (unlikely for two Geminis), the sex won't be satisfying. As a couple and as individuals, passion and attraction begin in the mind.

You're sure to have plenty of mutual interests, particularly anything that involves information and communication (books, movies, the Internet, writing) and no doubt have dozens of acquaintances and friends.

Gemini tends to be a high-energy sign, and with four of you to contend with in the relationship, nerves may get frazzled pretty easily. If you're involved with another Gemini, follow your mother's advice: Get plenty of rest, eat regular nutritious meals (as opposed to junk food on the run), and try to slow down your daily pace just a bit. Take time, as the saying goes, to smell the roses.

♋♋♋

CANCER COUPLE

In the unlikely event that you ever wonder who or what you're really about, head out to the beach and spend a few hours watching a crab, the creature that represents your sign. Notice its attachment to its home, its sideways movements, and how it avoids confrontation by sidling to the left or the right—unless it's cornered. Now apply these traits to you and your Cancerian partner.

There's no question that your home and home life are important to you both. You probably are happiest when you're snug as bugs and it's just the two of you. In some instances with Cancer couples, the closeness seems to bypass the necessity for language, as if they communicate telepathically. The challenge in this relationship, however, is that you don't like confrontation and will go to almost any length to avoid it. This can result in emotional wounds that fester over time.

If there are past-life connections between you and your Cancer, then you both may become aware of this most strongly during lovemaking. You may experience spontaneous memories from lives where you've been together. Feelings surface that puzzle you, mystify you. Pay attention. Figure it out together.

Although you and your Cancer partner undoubtedly agree on most things, you may disagree on issues related to your home. He may want the furniture arranged in one way, you in another. Or it may bug you that her toothbrush is always at the edge of the sink instead of in the holder. Small habits can be a bone of contention.

As a cardinal water sign, Cancer is in the domain of emotions, so it's important that you and your partner talk about feelings and that you're open enough with each other to express emotions—even negative emotions—openly and honestly. You both probably are nostalgic about some aspect of the past—childhoods, your mothers, your old neighborhoods—and it's important to share those memories. But don't obsess about them. Don't get stuck in the past. Most Cancers have a deep nostalgia about events in their pasts, but clinging to those memories, the good old days, or a relationship that went sour only holds you back. Seek always to live fully in the moment and to reach for the future.

When you're stressed as individuals or as a couple, head for water. A lake, a river, the ocean, or a salt marsh: It doesn't matter as long as your senses can soak up the flowing energy.

♌♌
LEO COUPLE

Imagine it. A pair of lions courting each other. It means lots of noise, posturing, and showy demonstrations. But once you get over that phase, the rest of the journey is about discovery. Your Leo partner provides you with the same qualities that you offer him or her—devotion, worship, loyalty, deep affection, and protection from anything and anyone who threatens to harm you.

Your sex life is probably quite active and satisfying. But it's important to remember that even though your partner shares your Sun sign, he or she isn't your clone and isn't here to idolize you, worship you, or bring you coffee in bed every morning. You may be a king or queen in your mind, but in the relationship, you must treat each other as equals.

Leos can be incredibly dramatic, vain, and egotistical, and if you're both acting out at the same time, it can wreck the relationship so completely that even the wreckage will be worthy of sociological comment. In the grander scheme of things, you may well be soul mates, but soul mates are first and foremost human beings. It's vital that you honor each other's differences as well as your similarities.

In a Leo partnership, creativity is important—your creative work as individuals as well as any creative projects you undertake together. Whether you're creating a family together or coauthoring a book, collaborating on a screenplay, or making a movie, your creative partnership is as vital to the health of the relationship as your sex life. Even if you butt heads on the specifics of the project—and you probably will—this is where the alchemy between you unfolds. This is where the two of you shine as a couple. If your creative interests take you on different paths, that's fine, too. You and your partner act as each other's support group, critic, and greatest fan.

In fact, the bottom line in a Leo partnership could be that you've come together in this life to explore your creative abilities as individuals and as a couple. It may not always be easy or simple, but it will never be boring.

♍ ♍

VIRGO COUPLE

Once upon a time, there were two little peas in a pod. They got along beautifully and saw eye to eye on just about everything. The only problem they had—and granted, it was minor, but so annoying at times—was that they picked on each other. It was never about huge issues, just the little things, such as "Why did you leave the top off the toothpaste?"

For every Virgo, some facet of your journey is about perfecting the self. As one Virgo friend put it, "I'm a work in progress." Even if you don't think of your quest for perfection as pertaining to you personally, that's really what it's about. So when two Virgos get together, the partnership itself becomes the work in progress and it's all too easy to pick on or criticize each other when things aren't, well, perfect!

You're both consummate communicators, though, and if you can steer clear of the petty criticisms and work on yourselves individually, this relationship can hum right along with only minor bumps. As mutable earth signs, your greatest strengths are that you both have discerning intellects and are masters of details. If these talents can come together in some sort of creative partnership, then there's little that you can't achieve together.

Some Virgos are worriers, and if one of you tends in that direction, then you may have stomach or digestion problems. If so, then look at it as a metaphor and ask yourself which experiences you are unable to digest or assimilate.

In a Virgo partnership, you both benefit from doing things for other people. It may be something as large as heading up a charitable organization or something as small as volunteering at a local animal shelter or answering a friend's midnight call for help. By turning your attention away from yourselves, each other, and the relationship, your quest for perfection embraces the larger world.

♎♎
LIBRA COUPLE

Balance is what you're looking for in this relationship, and it's probably the very thing that eludes you. But not to worry. When a couple of Libras get together, they're usually so anxious to please each other that ugly emotional issues rarely surface and confrontations are rare.

As cardinal air signs and the most social of the air signs, the two of you undoubtedly have numerous friends and acquaintances and spend a lot of your time socializing. When you're not with other people, you talk a lot to each other, discussing everything from art and music to your spiritual beliefs. Intellectual stimulation is vital to the health of your partnership and when it can be combined with a joint creative endeavor, everything between you flourishes.

Making decisions may be a challenge in this pairing. Neither of you is quick to make a decision because first you have to weigh all sides of the issues. It's easy for you both to slide into another person's skin and easier still to slide into each other's skins. You empathize so completely with the other person that you don't know which way to turn. But once you finally decide to go one way or another, you usually stick to it.

Art, music, and literature are likely to figure prominently in your relationship, and one of your favorite couple pastimes may be visiting art galleries. You both have a fondness for beautiful things—whether it's art or your own surroundings or just a pastoral countryside. And this translates into your emotional arena as a need for tranquility and peace in your domestic life. If you and your partner have children, particularly children whose Sun signs don't mesh well with your own, then there may be times when your domestic tranquility heads south. You both need some downtime to recoup your energy and recharge your creative batteries. With a little luck, you won't need downtime at the same time.

As two Venus-ruled individuals, it's crucial to keep the romance alive in your partnership. Part of the reason you've come together this time around, after all, is to learn that beauty, romance, and love are integral to a successful, creative partnership.

♏♏

SCORPIO COUPLE

This partnership is marked by emotional intensity. Of course, that won't bother either of you. You're both quite at home in the realm of emotions and thrive on intense experiences. This is great as long as the two of you are getting along. But in the event that you disagree over something, the repercussions can be quite severe. That stinger at the end of the symbol that represents your sign is quite literal. When you're crossed, you don't hesitate to get even, and you never forget a slight. So if you and your partner disagree, think twice before you voice your opinion. Unless it concerns an issue about which you feel very strongly, it might be best to keep your own counsel.

Scorpio has an inherent suspicion and distrust of most people, and it takes a long time to win your confidence. In a partnership, this could be a touchy area, as in "I love you but I don't trust you." Or, "Show me how much you love me by trusting me implicitly." You tend to live in a world of absolutes (while the rest of us slog along in a world made up of shades of gray) and as long as your partner does, too, then your problems should be minimal. But if either of you ever breaches the other's trust, don't expect to be forgiven. That breach will end the relationship.

Scorpio, as a fixed water sign ruled by powerful Pluto, always has strong opinions and, like Taurus, is slow to change his mind. If you and your partner have the same or similar opinions on the important stuff, then you support each other in your life choices. But if your opinions and beliefs are fundamentally different, then you may have problems before the relationship even gets out of the gate.

Your sex life is never about just sex; it's one way of communicating with each other at the deepest, most psychic level. As long as your sex life is satisfying to you both, then it's likely everything else will roll along fairly smoothly.

SAGITTARIUS COUPLE

There are few if any couples who have more fun than these two. That's only fitting for a sign ruled by jolly Jupiter, the Santa Claus of the zodiac.

You and your partner, in fact, were probably drawn to each other's mutual love of life, philosophies, and spiritual beliefs; your quests for truth and adventure; and/or your love of travel. There isn't any lack of communication in your relationship, but you're both so eager at times to say what you need to say that you may fail to really listen to each other.

Sagittarians are usually idealists and these ideals can run the gamut—animal rights to feeding the hungry to some spiritual cause. If you and your partner share similar ideals, then your relationship is just that much stronger. This is also an independent sign, so your partner probably won't be offended if you spend an evening out with your friends. But your partner may not be quite so understanding if you decide to head off for the African bush without him or her. After all, your fellow Sadge is just as avid a traveler as you are.

If both of you are gamblers and risk takers, as many Sagittarians are, then you should have some money stashed away in case some of the risks don't pan out. But you tend to be lucky, probably because all that Jupiter energy fills you with an unflappable optimism and belief in your own abilities. On the rare occasion when you or your partner is mired in a black mood, it doesn't last long. You pick yourselves up, dust yourselves off, and head out for the next gamble, the next risk, the next adventure.

The major pitfalls in this partnership are the same pitfalls that all Sagittarians face—self-righteousness. You figure you have the edge on truth, whether it's spiritual truth or just plain old truth about what's really going on. If you and your partner are on opposing sides of whatever triggers an attitude of "I'm right and you're wrong," then sparks are going to fly.

♑ ♑

CAPRICORN COUPLE

As a cardinal earth sign ruled by Saturn, a relationship between two Capricorns can be very serious business. You're equally ambitious, and if that ambition can be combined in a joint business venture of some kind, there will be no happier couple!

You both have an extremely practical side to your personalities and it's unlikely you'll disagree on anything concerning finances. Capricorns are adept at manifesting what they need and desire, and perhaps one of you needs to learn from the other just how easy it is. Even though you both are probably very responsible about stashing money away for the future, be sure to keep some money aside to enjoy today. In fact, the point of that statement is to enjoy. All too frequently, you may forget that life isn't just about work and achievement. It's also about enjoyment.

Capricorn usually isn't associated with heightened sexuality, but this earth sign can be fiercely passionate and sexual. The challenge in the partnership may be learning how to balance your sexual attraction to each other with the other demands in your life! Although you probably aren't the jealous type, you and your partner may well be possessive of each other. To some extent, this depends on your age and your experiences in other relationships. But just keep that in mind because it could have a bearing at some point on the health of the relationship.

Humor will get you through any rough spots or hassles in the partnership. Chances are that either you or your partner or perhaps both of you have a wry sense of humor that other people may not even understand. But who cares, right? It's as if your partnership has its own secret language, complete with codes—a look, a touch, a line you hear that cracks you both up at the same time and leaves everyone else scratching their heads in puzzlement. But that's the beauty of it all!

AQUARIUS COUPLE

You love and respect each other and get along great, but you're both so busy saving the world that you may not have a whole lot of time to spend with each other. One of you may be taking workshops and seminars on anything from alternative healing to yoga, and the other one is off trying to solve the ET issue once and for all.

Ordinary life bores Aquarius. You seek the odd, the eccentric, the decidedly different, so it makes sense, even to an Aquarian, to get involved with another Aquarian. That pretty much ensures that you'll never be bored, that you will always have a companion with whom you can engage in lively discussions, and that at least one person in the universe will understand your quirks.

But all of the above is necessary and vital in the Aquarian equation for happiness.

However—and here's the caveat—you're a fixed sign, often as stubborn as Taurus, and when you put two fixed signs together for any length of time, you invariably reach the point where one or the other refuses to bend. You may feel, "We have to do this my way or I refuse to change my mind." In a partnership, this kind of obstinacy can be a major problem, even between two people who honor individual differences.

Sex in an Aquarian partnership is likely to be as idiosyncratic as everything else in your relationship. One thing is for certain, though. Both of you must be seduced intellectually, through ideas, possibilities, or visions of what might be, before your bodies even enter the picture. But once that mental connection is established, the rest of the journey unfolds according to a rhythm that only the two of you understand. And that's just fine, right?

PISCES COUPLE

While the Aquarian couple is lost in discourse on how to improve the world, the Piscean couple is swimming through the clear, silent waters of their collective imaginations, intuitions, and feelings. Like Gemini, this sign is symbolized by two of something—a pair of fish swimming in opposite directions—so there are really four of you to contend with in this partnership. The foursome may not be as glaringly apparent as it is for a Gemini couple, but it's there, and it can certainly be challenging.

This mutable water sign is sometimes associated with escapism through drugs or alcohol, a byproduct of your Neptune ruler. But Neptune also rules the imagination and higher inspiration, so it's equally possible that you and your Pisces partner can enjoy a creative and imaginative relationship.

One of the strengths in this pairing is a communication that at times seems telepathic. You complete each other's sentences, think of the same thing at the same moment, or know when your partner is on the other end of a ringing phone. Given this strong bond, it's likely that when you meet each other, the attraction will be powerfully visceral and that one or both of you will recognize a soul mate.

Pisces is a gentle, compassionate sign and, like Scorpio and Sagittarius, is often linked to spirituality. Part of this may be that the fish is a symbol associated with Christianity. But the truth is even simpler: Pisceans usually have rich, fecund inner lives and, through their intuition and imagination, are able to delve into areas that may elude the rest of us. So it's possible that spirituality may be a central theme in your relationship.

A possible challenge in this pairing is that Pisces sometimes plays a martyr or savior role, and if you're both playing this role at the same time, the results could be harmful.

Sun/North Node
Connections

Whenever there's a conjunction between your Sun and your partner's North Node or vice versa, then pay attention. The relationship is an important one and this type of conjunction describes your path as a couple—the strengths and challenges both individuals face and how you and your partner evolve through the relationship to achieve your individual potential.

Let's take an example. Actress Susan Sarandon has a Libra Sun. Her partner, actor and director Tim Robbins, also has a Libra Sun, and his North Node is in Libra. This indicates that she helps him through the creative self-expression of her Sun sign to achieve his potential and to evolve spiritually. His North Node, in turn, helps her push the envelope of her own abilities. Not surprisingly, their creative partnership resulted in an Oscar for Sarandon for *Dead Man Walking*, which Robbins directed. They are among the most politically outspoken couples in Hollywood, evident in the house placement of their Sun/Node contact—the ninth house, symbolic of one's worldview. The fact that the contact is in Libra is also quite telling. What is Libra if not the sign of justice and balance?

Because the North and South Nodes always form an axis, it means that a South Node falls opposite a North Node. So if you have your North Node in Aries, your South Node will be in Libra, exactly 180 degrees away. Suppose your or your partner's Sun is conjunct with the other person's South Node? Does the meaning change? You bet. It's usually indicative of a strong past-life connection. There's probably a powerful attraction between you and the other person. In close relationships, such as in a family, if you share a South Node/Sun connection with a parent or sibling, you should develop an awareness about what that connection means and how that individual represents the qualities you must grow beyond in this life. But there's more about this particular configuration in chapter 11.

By now you should have a pretty good idea of what the signs mean, so I've described the conjunctions by house placement. When reading through the descriptions, always put the other person's Sun or North Node in the appropriate house in *your* chart, as you did in the explanation at the beginning of part two. Then your partner can put your Sun or North Node in the appropriate house in *his or her* chart. That way you both glean information from the descriptions.

FIRST HOUSE COUPLE

Your Karmic Path: As a couple, there's a lot of creative give and take between you. One or both of you may have had lessons to learn in childhood concerning authority and/or your father. You've come together to explore the vast potential of the self and to support each other's need to learn independence. Together, you are trailblazers.

Strength: You nurture and support each other's energies and endeavors and help clarify each other's goals.

Challenge: Independence may be a thorny issue. One of you may be too willing to give in to the other.

SECOND HOUSE COUPLE

Your Karmic Path: You define your values as a couple separate from those of your families and peers, and you grow through achieving financial prosperity. You both may be workaholics, but at least you're working toward common goals. One or both of you may have an interest in metaphysics and be deeply intuitive. You're able to use your intuition in the financial arena.

Strength: You learn from each other in the financial arena.

Challenge: Making time for each other may be your greatest challenge.

THIRD HOUSE COUPLE

Your Karmic Path: You help each other define what restricts your physical or intellectual freedom. Through the relationship, you learn to communicate what you think and feel when you think and feel it—instead of after the fact. Siblings, relatives, and neighbors play important karmic roles in your lives. One or both of you have a solid worldview and belief system that helps you achieve your soul's agenda.

Strength: Your ability to communicate with each other is your greatest strength.

Challenge: The tug of an ephemeral notion of freedom may keep one or both of you from committing fully to the relationship.

FOURTH HOUSE COUPLE

Your Karmic Path: As a couple, your greatest opportunities for spiritual growth occur through your home life. Home and family roots are important to the relationship. You support each other's career endeavors and achievements, while reminding each other that home is where the heart is. Your personal life is the bedrock from which all else flows.

Strength: With a solid home life, everything else in life flows more easily.

Challenge: One of you may feel torn between home and career.

FIFTH HOUSE COUPLE

Your Karmic Path: You've come together to explore your creative potential and abilities as a couple. This includes children and any kind of creative endeavor. Your greatest spiritual growth occurs through creative self-expression. Your romance is kept alive through your joint creative expression and your genuine enjoyment of each other's company.

Strength: Your combined intuitive abilities lead you in the direction that is right for you as a couple and as individuals.

Challenge: Because the fifth house also represents romance, speculation, and pleasure, there's a temptation to fritter away your talents.

SIXTH HOUSE COUPLE

Your Karmic Path: You've come together this time around to remind each other to use what you've learned in other lives in a concrete way, on a daily basis. This can involve the use of healing and intuitive talents or being of service to others out of compassion and desire rather than because of personal compensation. Although you do some of your best work in solitude, try not to become reclusive in your partnership.

Strength: You're able to combine your energies to create a daily atmosphere in which you both flourish spiritually.

Challenge: Lack of self-discipline may be your biggest challenge.

SEVENTH HOUSE COUPLE

Your Karmic Path: Your partnership is an entity unto itself. Together, you learn to put individual concerns aside and do what is best for the success of the relationship. Your highest achievements and greatest prosperity come through joint endeavors. You're together to learn cooperation and to act as each other's support system.

Strength: You evolve through marriage and committed partnerships.

Challenge: Maintaining the balance in the relationship without either of your sacrificing your own needs and desires is a challenge for both of you.

EIGHTH HOUSE COUPLE

Your Karmic Path: This time around, you've come together to share your resources with each other and with other people. Your combined free will is an enormously powerful force and can bring about great change—if you let it. Your interest in metaphysical topics and issues is part of your ongoing investigation into the hidden areas of life.

Strength: You and your partner have an excellent grasp of public opinion. Use it in whatever you do.

Challenge: One or both of you may forget that this lifetime together is about cooperation.

NINTH HOUSE COUPLE

Your Karmic Path: You're together to explore worldviews that differ greatly from your own. This may include extensive foreign travel or involvement in publishing, higher education, and/or spiritual study. In a sense, you're searching to define your joint mythology, who you both are (and what your relationship is) in terms of the larger collective of humanity. Spiritual beliefs are important to you both.

Strength: As a couple, your greatest spiritual growth lies in the development of your higher mind.

Challenge: It's easy to slide back into old thought patterns that inhibit your growth.

TENTH HOUSE COUPLE

Your Karmic Path: Your path is about achievement. It's that simple—and that complex. You nurture and feed each other's ambitions and professional achievements. Serendipity plays a big role in your scheme of things as a couple. Together, you can build an empire or an organization that brings about great, positive change in the world.

Strength: You have clear goals and ambitions.

Challenge: You may feel torn between your obligations to your family and to your career.

ELEVENTH HOUSE COUPLE

Your Karmic Path: As a couple, you gain through your friends and group associations. In turn, your friends and acquaintances gain through their association with you and your partner. Your network supports your creative dreams and even helps you achieve them.

Strength: You understand the pulse of public opinion and the spiritual communion that occurs in the best of friendships.

Challenge: Selfish attitudes may surface concerning your or your partner's pleasures and creativity.

TWELFTH HOUSE COUPLE

Your Karmic Path: Through profound inner work that you engage in as a couple, you gain understanding about yourself, each other, and the larger cosmos of which you're a part. If one or both of you have disowned personal power, you help each other recover it and use it to achieve your creative and spiritual potential.

Strength: Your combined intuition is a powerful force.

Challenge: One or both of you seek escapism.

EQUALS

ONE SIGN APART

When signs are separated by thirty degrees, the aspect is called a semisextile, a fancy name for the sign that's your next-door neighbor. If you're a Cancer, then your neighbor is either a Gemini or a Leo. If you're an Aquarius, your neighbor is either a Capricorn or a Pisces. This aspect is considered a weak one by most astrologers, with not much going for it in terms of Sun sign compatibility. The elements and qualities in such pairings are always at odds, and the archetypal energy for the signs don't have much in common. So what makes these relationships work?

It could be that because the respective Sun signs are far enough apart, the couple has other planets in common. Or perhaps the couple simply has to work harder to make the relationship succeed. Whatever the attraction, a semisextile relationship appears to involve a conscious choice, and sometimes one individual gives up something to be in the relationship.

The most notable example is that of the Duke and Duchess of Windsor (Cancer and Gemini). He chose to give up the throne so that he could marry her. Percy Bysshe Shelley (Leo) eloped with Mary Godwin

(Virgo) while he was still married to his first wife. After his first wife drowned herself, Percy was denied custody of his children because he was a professed atheist. He married Mary when she was eighteen, and she was widowed six years later when Percy drowned during a storm.

Other semisextile partnerships include Nicole Kidman (Gemini) and Tom Cruise (Cancer), and Paul Newman (Aquarius) and Joanne Woodward (Pisces).

Astrologer Linda Goodman seemed to have a theory about these next-door neighbor relationships. She claimed the sign right before yours represents the sign you were in your most recent past life and, at some level, each of us has memories about that life. Maybe it's true. Who knows? Who can say for sure?

Goodman sometimes referred to these combinations as teacher/ student relationships, and perhaps thirty years ago they were. But we've entered a new century, with gender roles far less clearly defined than they once were, and to me, these combinations are about equals. Despite glaring differences, couples who are zodiac neighbors need to be regarded as equals in their partnerships. "I don't do the dishes or cook dinner just because I'm the woman." Or, "Just because I'm the guy doesn't mean I take the car in for an oil change."

I've known a number of partners who fall into the equals category, and often their roles are completely nontraditional. Even if they were raised in traditional households—a mom at home, a dad who left for work every day—those traditions don't seem to hold true for them. Of course, the world has changed significantly since the days of *Leave It to Beaver*. Women comprise a major part of the workforce, and many working families need two paychecks to make it. Kids of divorced parents often split their time between two families, providing them with ample opportunities to observe how different family units work or don't work.

My husband and I fall into this category. He has a Sun and North Node in Taurus and I have a Sun and North Node in Gemini, and our family structure is nontraditional. We both work at home. Rob is the cook (probably out of self-defense!), and we share household responsibilities. My daughter was probably around twelve when she came home one day exclaiming, "Mom, I thought everyone's Dad was the cook in the family!"

Sun Sign Combinations

This section describes how you and your partner relate to each other.

♈♉

ARIES/TAURUS COUPLE

On the surface, it seems these two signs have absolutely nothing in common. Aries is a cardinal fire sign and Taurus, fixed earth. And yet, Aries is ruled by Mars and Taurus is ruled by Venus, the two planets that represent male and female.

Both signs are independent and seek a relationship between equals, so each person is free to develop individual interests and creative passions. If Aries leads the way in some joint creative project or endeavor, then Taurus can be depended upon to finish it. When Aries rushes forth impatiently, Taurus reins in all that impatient energy and slows things down to a manageable level. But it works in reverse, too. When Taurus is moving too slowly, Aries sweeps through and gets the bull moving again. If Taurus is stuck in the rut of routine, Aries races in and jerks Taurus off in some new, exciting direction. A fine balance, perhaps, but a good one when it's finally mastered.

Taurus tends to be more reticent than Aries, a potential problem that can reach mammoth proportions if Aries is in a boastful "Me Me" mode. The other potential problem area is finances. Aries usually is an impulsive spender—"I want it, I'll buy it, and I'll do it now"—whereas Taurus is cautious, happy to save and pay cash for whatever it is. However, Taurus loves beautiful things and isn't adverse to buying big ticket items on credit. Both have tempers, but it takes Taurus longer to blow and when it comes, clear the decks. Even Aries may be intimidated.

Despite differences, passionate Aries and sensuous Taurus get along just fine in the bedroom.

♉ ♊
TAURUS/GEMINI COUPLE

Taurus moves slowly; Gemini is lightning quick. Taurus is fixed earth, practical yet sensual, firmly rooted in the physical world. Gemini is mutable air, lives in the world of ideas, and generally isn't practical at all. One is ruled by Venus, the other by Mercury. So what's the attraction?

It may be that simple yet complex quality called balance. When Taurus craves diversity and excitement, Gemini provides it. When Gemini's restless energy desperately needs grounding and time out, Taurus opens the door to the garden and invites Gemini to sit in the sunlight for a while and smell the flowers. Gemini is attracted to the bull's stability, and Taurus is attracted to the twins' dexterity with words and ideas. Taurus may be puzzled by the mercurial mood swings in a Gemini, but the bull will never be bored. Geminis may be mystified by the bull's quiet stillness, but it will be a constant source of fascination.

Problem areas? Well, there are several possibilities. Gemini is a communicator, and Taurus is the strong, silent type. It's infuriating for a Gemini to be met with cool detachment when he or she wants to have a conversation about ideas, feelings, or anything else. It's equally frustrating for a Taurus to have a partner badgering him or her when the bull just wants to chill. Another potential problem is finances. When Gemini thinks about the future, it's usually not in terms of retirement and financial stability. Taurus sees stability in saving and Gemini sees restriction.

But perhaps this combination works precisely because of the individual differences.

♊♋
GEMINI/CANCER COUPLE

Mutable air and cardinal water: That combination may, on the surface, seem even stranger than the previous one. After all, what could social butterfly and communicator Gemini have in common with moody, imaginative Cancer?

Quite a bit, actually.

Both signs are taciturn, given to strange and abrupt shifts in their moods. Cancer is rarely put off by Gemini's mercurial shifts and doesn't worry too much about which twin is in charge on a given day. Gemini understands Cancer's moodiness but may be put off by the crab's reluctance to talk about the source of the mood. Gemini and Cancer are both terrific storytellers and have good imaginations. Where Gemini often tells a story as a way of imparting information, Cancer tells a story to impart an emotion or intuitive knowledge. Either way, the end result is the same: People listen raptly. When these two tell stories to each other, the rest of the world drops away.

As a cardinal sign, Cancer is far more single-minded and tenacious than Gemini is. The crab clings tightly to whatever it values and to everything that makes it feel secure and comfortable—the good old days, home, possessions, property or money, even people. This can be a potential problem for Gemini, who may cling to ideas but rarely to people. On the other hand, Gemini's flexibility sometimes proves just a tad too flexible for Cancer's tastes, particularly when it smacks of unreliability. "But we made plans," Cancer says. "You made plans," Gemini replies. "I didn't."

Still, there's something about this combination that each sign gravitates toward. Perhaps, when all it said and done, Cancer brings Gemini more into alignment with his or her emotions and Gemini ignites Cancer's intuitive mind.

♋♌
CANCER/LEO COUPLE

The ruling planets for these two signs really do tell the story: The Moon rules Cancer, and the Sun rules Leo. You can't get much more yin and yang than that. So how does this combination work at all?

Easy. Leo, fixed fire, is always aware that water puts out fire. Of course, it's not quite that simple, so let's take a deeper look.

One thing that's needed for this combination to work over a period of time is self-awareness. Even though Cancer may enjoy Leo's high-voltage energy and Leo, on downtime, certainly enjoys Cancer's immersion in the waters of the self, it's necessary to stay on top of the relationship for this combination to succeed over a period of time. Here's why.

Leo can be arrogant and selfish and always wants the spotlight. Cancer likes the spotlight, too, but pretends otherwise and then suffers in silence, resentment growing like a malignant tumor. Or here's another possibility: Cancer's emotions and concern over stability completely squash Leo's love of life and generosity. Fortunately, there's another scenario: Cancer's strong intuitive and imaginative nature melds with Leo's creative drive and the two produce something far greater than either of them could produce alone.

Another potentially troubling area is finances. Cancer, like Taurus, often views money in the bank as security. But Leo, who can be as impulsive a spender as Aries is, scoffs and says, "Hey, there's more where that came from." While a belief in the universe's abundance is always admirable, Cancer probably won't buy it.

However, if these two can give each other enough room and learn to accommodate each other's differences, this relationship can work for the long haul.

♌♍
LEO/VIRGO COUPLE

Leo: "The gall, the prissy, exacting gall…"
Virgo: "The unbridled arrogance…"
Leo, fixed fire, and Virgo, mutable earth, are coming at life from

different ends of the continuum. With Leo, it's showtime! Bring out the audience, the lights, the stage, and watch Leo rise to the occasion and shine. Leo wants to be applauded and recognized for everything he or she does. Virgo prefers to remain in the background, quietly watching, absorbing, fitting the pieces of the puzzle together, tending to details. And yet, neither description is the full story for these two dynamic signs.

Leo also can be a powerful leader and organizer, galvanizing the troops into action for whatever purpose. While the lion's ego must always be fed, inside him or her waits a quiet child, arms outstretched, whispering, "Appreciate me. Love me." Virgo hears those whispers and accommodates Leo—but only to a point. Virgo won't wait on the lion, won't worship at his or her feet. Virgo may even criticize the lion—big mistake—but when all is said and done, Virgo's interest is in the inner person. Virgo asks, "Who are you when you aren't playing to your audience?"

When these two learn how to work with each other's differences, this combination holds positive surprises. Creatively, the two can accomplish a great deal. Leo makes the contacts and draws the mass support needed for whatever the creative endeavor might be, and Virgo tends to all the details, perfecting the project, fitting the pieces together. Virgo also brings an inner illumination to any creative project, a kind of intuitive savvy that Leo certainly should heed.

♍ ♎

VIRGO/LIBRA COUPLE

Both signs are fundamentally peaceful, with a profound dislike of harmony and tumult. Libra, in particular, becomes deeply troubled by disharmony in his or her personal life and will often do anything to keep the peace, even distort the truth. Virgo rarely distorts the truth, even to keep the peace, but will resort to sharp criticism. "You didn't dot the I." It can be as petty as that. But more often than not, Virgo's criticisms target the self. "I'm not good enough, smart enough, cute enough."

It's not that Virgo is mean-spirited or a masochist. The Virgo soul is inherently gentle. But it's this thing Virgo has for perfection, which is ultimately the perfection of the self, as though Virgo sees his or her soul as a diamond in the rough. Or a diamond still buried in stone. Libra isn't too concerned about diamonds, unless they're already polished and stunning, and then he or she admires the finished product with an artist's eye. And that's the wonder of Libra.

Everything a Libra perceives and experiences is done so through the honed sensibilities of an artist—and it doesn't matter whether the Libra is actually an artist or a writer or a musician. He or she may well be an accountant. The point is that Libra sees beauty where Virgo may see lack of order or small imperfections.

However, when these two figure out all these differences and decide to commit in spite of them, the relationship works. Virgo's presence soothes, Libra's presence creates beauty, and the music these two create together can knock your socks off.

♎ ♏

LIBRA/SCORPIO COUPLE

The Scorpio quest ultimately ends up as a search for the absolute bottom line. The Libra quest is always about fairness and balance. So when these two come together, their journey is marked by discovery.

The discovery centers on several areas. Scorpio, who lives in a black and white world where things are either right or wrong, is mystified by Libra's ability to see the many sides of an issue. "How can anyone argue so convincingly on either side of the fence?" Scorpio wonders. Libra admires Scorpio's tenacity, that ability to keep after something—a person, topic, political office, job, feeling, or hunch—until it's grasped. But really, Libra asks, "What's the point when the obstacles seem to be stacking up so quickly?"

When Libra is racked by indecision, Scorpio steps in with a pep talk that can be summed up in a few words: "Make up your mind one way or another!" When Scorpio brews and mulls in sullenness, Libra steps in with that sunny optimism: "Hey, it's never as bad as it seems."

"Yeah, it's worse than it seems," Scorpio thinks. But some of that Libra optimism manages to shine through the cracks in the Scorpion's armor.

The dichotomies in this relationship are glaring. But the differences find their own balance in a way no one else but these two can understand. The Scorpion's armor hides a deep sensitivity and intuition that grasps what the logical mind can't, and Scorpio must exercise both in a relationship with Libra. Sexually, things work very well with these two, and lovemaking often compensates for some of their differences.

♏ ♐
SCORPIO/SAGITTARIUS COUPLE

Here it is in a nutshell: With Sagittarius, what you see is what you get. With Scorpio, what you see definitely isn't all you get. And that's the heart of the combination's dilemma.

But let's take a deeper look. Scorpio is secretive and Sagittarius is about as upfront and blunt as anyone can be. Scorpio digs and digs to find answers; Sagittarius is interested in the Big Picture and doesn't really think too much about answers. Sagittarius, ruled by jolly Jupiter, has an abundance of optimism and good cheer, plus a grand sense of adventure; Scorpio, ruled by transformative Pluto, is perpetually braced against the unknown. So where's the bridge that allows these two to relate to each other at all?

Well, at the risk of sounding banal, the bridge is love.

Scorpio's passions are profound and powerful and Sagittarius's passions are huge, expansive, and all-encompassing. When these forces converge because both individuals are on a spiritual or creative quest, the combined energy is explosive enough to satisfy both of them. It's then that Scorpio learns to trust and Sagittarius learns to tone down his or her bluntness. It's then that they realize they won't settle for anything less than equality. Why should they? Why should anyone?

And so, in the evolution of the partnership, Sagittarius observes how Scorpio's powerful will can manifest and create whatever is needed. In turn, Scorpio observes how Sagittarius's infinite capacity for trust and faith can turn events on a dime.

↗ ♑
SAGITTARIUS/CAPRICORN COUPLE

Once upon a time, there was a centaur who wandered the world in search of truth. He came upon a goat high up on a lonely, windy mountainside and asked the goat where it was headed. "To the top of the mountain, of course."

"What's at the top?" the centaur asked.

"I don't know. I'm not there yet."

"Then why do you want to get there?"

"Because that's my goal."

Capricorn sets a goal and strives to attain it, and it doesn't matter whether it takes the goat sixty days or sixty years to do it. One way or another, Capricorn attains the goal and then sets another. Life is a series of carefully achieved steps on a ladder that lead to the top. Sagittarius, looking for nothing less than the truth, is puzzled by this part of the Capricorn psyche. Yet, at the same time, Sadge is dazzled because Capricorn seems so self-assured and certain, so confident of his or her ability to get to the top of that mountain.

In Sagittarians who aren't self-aware, this search for truth can collapse into self-righteousness, particularly when organized religion is part of the equation. Capricorn, who respects authority, may get suckered into the religious thing and Sadge, seeing an opportunity to deter Capricorn from this ridiculous climb up the mountain, uses it for control. Capricorn, reluctant to rock the boat, may put up with the situation for a while, but eventually the top of that mountain beckons again and the goat breaks free.

But the idealism and honesty of an evolved Sagittarius appeal to the Capricorn spirit because in that long trek up the mountain Capricorn needs to be reminded that the goal isn't really the point. The journey is what matters. And the journey is something Sagittarius knows a lot about.

♑ ♒♒
CAPRICORN/AQUARIUS COUPLE

Before the discovery of Uranus, Capricorn and Aquarius shared the same ruler, Saturn. It's now considered to be the coruler of Aquarius, so these two signs share certain attributes, although an adherence to tradition isn't among them.

Aquarius is quirky and individualistic and definitely doesn't function according to any standard that Capricorn finds attractive or reasonable. Most Aquarians tend to create their own rules, philosophies, and belief systems and really don't care how far out of the mainstream they are. Capricorns, though, are concerned about rules, regulations, and family and societal traditions. Aquarius can be more practical than either Gemini or Libra is, but he certainly can't beat out the pragmatism of the typical Capricorn.

Again, blame their respective rulers. Saturn governs the rules of physical reality and Uranus governs intuition, genius, abrupt and unexpected change, and all individual idiosyncratic behavior. While Capricorn is putting in sixteen-hour days at work, Aquarius is figuring out the riddle of the universe or dabbling in esoterica—reincarnation, astrology, UFOs, things that go bump in the night. Yet, Aquarius, a fixed air sign, has the same tenacity as that of Taurus and Scorpio, the other fixed signs. When it suits the water bearer, he or she gathers facts, digs for information, and bases decisions on what is learned. But the intuitive brilliance of the sign allows these individuals to bypass what's immaterial.

When a Capricorn understands all this about his or her Aquarian mate, then the goat can take all these brilliant insights and help make them practical and useful. And because Capricorn is proficient at multitasking, he or he can do this while climbing the mountain toward the summit of his own ambitions.

This pairing probably works best when both individuals are older, past the age of thirty-five.

♒♓
AQUARIUS/PISCES COUPLE

Zany Aquarius and dreamy Pisces get along quite well, once they have jumped through the usual hoops that air and water signs seem to go through when they find themselves involved with each other. Pisces is more driven by emotions and Aquarius by the mind, but on an intuitive level they are evenly matched because Pisces is usually so psychic.

Both are idiosyncratic, but in different ways. While Aquarius is roaming through the realm of ideas, future trends, and possibilities, Pisces is swimming through the vastness of his or her own imagination. When Aquarius bluntly asks to find out whatever he or she wants to know, Pisces simply intuits. When these two combine their efforts in a creative endeavor—whether it's child rearing or writing the great American novel—they tend to work well together.

The major problem area with this combination is emotions. Aquarius detaches from the world of feeling with complete ease, but Pisces is driven by emotion. When Pisces craves affection and company, Aquarius may be off investigating the latest UFO sighting. Pisces individuals get their feelings hurt easily, but you can say almost anything to Aquarians and they shrug it off.

Aquarius is moved emotionally by the sight of a homeless beggar on the street and feels compelled to donate money to a charity that helps homeless beggars. But when Pisces sees that same homeless beggar, he or she wants to bring the beggar home, educate and feed him, and get him back on his feet again. The Piscean compassion is empathic; the Aquarian compassion is intellectual.

Pisces is sometimes much too accommodating and, when involved with a fire sign or with powerful fixed signs (Scorpio, Aquarius), should be cautious in that sense. For a Pisces, the line between accommodation and victimization is very thin.

♓♈
PISCES/ARIES COUPLE

Whew. Forget the water and fire elements with this combination. It's really about the planets that rule these signs—Neptune and Mars. Neptune rules the oceans, poetry, and our illusions, higher inspiration, imagination, and desire for escapism. Mars rules war, the military, surgery, and our physical and sexual energy. So what can these two signs possibly have in common?

Not much.

Aries is aggressive; Pisces tends to be passive. Aries can be enormously selfish, egotistical, and impatient, and believes—often rightly so—that he or she can do anything. Pisces is gentle, compassionate, artistic, secretive, and elusive. But when these two find a middle ground where they can coexist, the relationship works, particularly with an Aries man and a Pisces woman. The Piscean woman softens the Aries man, smoothing the rough, abrasive edges and tempering his impatience. In turn, the Aries man builds enthusiasm in Pisces, urging her to seize her dreams, try new things, and move in new, unexplored directions. When the relationship involves a Pisces man and an Aries woman, she tends to walk all over him.

In self-aware people, however, there's a recognition between these two of past-life connections that often speak louder than any present differences. Due to the psychic perceptions of most Pisces, this sign is very likely to feel the tug of past-life relationships. And once Pisces feels that tug, images of the past life may surface. Soul mate or adversary? Parent or child? Teacher or student? Pisces always seems to intuit exactly what he or she needs to know about the conditions of a past-life relationship.

When both individuals in this partnership are self-aware and able to find a middle ground, they develop a strong inner rapport that may be hard for the rest of us to fathom but which works just fine for them.

Sun/North Node
Connections

The descriptions below address both variations of a combination. If you have a first house Sun and your partner's North Node falls in your second house, or if your Sun is in the second house and your partner's North Node falls in your first, then the first description applies to both.

The Sun/North Node combinations describe your path as a couple—the strengths and challenges you face in the relationship and how you and your partner evolve through the partnership to achieve your individual potentials. However, you can apply the descriptions to anyone in your life.

When astrologers compare a couple's chart, they often use the biwheel technique that we explored at the beginning of part two. This enables you to see where your partner's planets fall in your houses and which of your planets are hit. The ways in which your partner's planets impact yours describes what your partner brings to the relationship. When your partner's chart is in the inner wheel and yours is in the biwheel, the planets indicate what you bring to your partner in the relationship.

Always start with your natal Sun and your own chart.

FIRST HOUSE/SECOND HOUSE COUPLE

Your Karmic Path: Through self-expression and personal effort, you and your partner help each other define and hone your individual values, even if those values differ. Your combined willpower, if you can harness it, is a force to be reckoned with. Your spiritual growth as a couple unfolds through allowing each other the freedom to develop individual talents and abilities, then using them in a cooperative way.

Strengths: You have a firm foundation on which to build your lives together.

Challenge: One of you is a workaholic who may forget what life is really about.

SECOND HOUSE/THIRD HOUSE COUPLE

Your Karmic Path: Communication figures prominently in your relationship. It helps you define your goals individually and as a couple and focus on the values that you have in common. For one or both of you, relationships with siblings, relatives, and neighbors are important. One of you finds solace and comfort in a certain spiritual belief system that may hold you back until you can communicate what you have learned. Education is crucial to the success of this relationship.

Strengths: You're in this journey together, as equals.

Challenge: At times, one of you believes he or she has the corner on truth.

THIRD HOUSE/FOURTH HOUSE COUPLE

Your Karmic Path: Your lives are structured around your families—birth families and adult families—and often includes siblings, relatives, and neighbors who are like family. As a couple, career may take a back seat to family life. Education is emphasized. Your communication skills as a couple are strong, and you're both happiest with some type of home-based business. Frequent moves is a possibility.

Strength: You know your priorities. Your family and home life provide the best opportunities for spiritual growth.

Challenge: One of you may be dogmatic about spiritual beliefs.

FOURTH HOUSE/FIFTH HOUSE COUPLE

Your Karmic Path: As a couple, family, roots, and creativity are important to you. You grow spiritually by developing and expressing your creativity and by supporting each other's creative aspirations. For one or both of you, children may figure prominently in the overall scheme of your lives.

Strengths: You're fully supportive of each other's creative endeavors.

Challenge: One of you may take speculative or romantic risks that undermine what you're trying to build together.

FIFTH HOUSE/SIXTH HOUSE COUPLE

Your Karmic Path: Your daily life together is important. It's possible that you are business partners or involved in creative work together. Health issues may be explored together—health maintenance; the inter-relationship between mind, body, and spirit; or alternative health. Children are a part of this equation, either your own or through work that you do with kids.

Strengths: You support each other's creative work.

Challenge: One of you feels more comfortable working with group creativity than working solo. This, in turn, can be problematic for the other partner because friends seem to be a third presence in the relationship.

SIXTH HOUSE/SEVENTH HOUSE COUPLE

Your Karmic Path: This combination emphasizes the partnership in all facets of daily life. You evolve spiritually as a couple when you consider what is good for the relationship, as opposed to what is good just for you or just for your partner. There's a strong intuitive understanding of how to keep your physical bodies healthy and the links between body, mind, and spirit.

Strength: Your greatest achievements come through your joint efforts.

Challenge: There can be an element of self-sacrifice in this combination because one partner may subjugate his or own desires and needs.

SEVENTH HOUSE/EIGHTH HOUSE COUPLE

Your Karmic Path: Through your partnership, you learn to share your resources. This combination can lead to an exploration of metaphysics, mythology, and all things mystical. Your mutual exploration of these areas can lead to a refinement and expansion of your spiritual beliefs.

Strength: Your partnership and metaphysical exploration create lasting bonds.

Challenge: Past-life issues may surface more easily in this combination, and those issues will have to be dealt with this time around. Any combination that involves the eighth house is likely to bring past-life issues to the surface.

EIGHT HOUSE/NINTH HOUSE COUPLE

Your Karmic Path: As a couple, you evolve spiritually and intuitively through your interactions with other people and by sharing your resources with them. Your spiritual beliefs are an integral part of the partnership. Higher education; publishing; foreign travel; and other countries, cultures, and peoples may play crucial roles.

Strength: You're both seekers and your quest is intended to expand your worldview.

Challenge: One of you draws strict boundaries between self and others or gets stuck in a limiting worldview.

NINTH HOUSE/TENTH HOUSE COUPLE

Your Karmic Path: Careers and worldviews play into this equation. There may be a tug of war between your domestic obligations and those of your careers or your higher education. Your combined spiritual beliefs may differ radically from the beliefs you grew up with as a child.

Strength: You evolve together into something larger than either of you can achieve alone.

Challenge: One of you may feel a deep nomadic restlessness to be on the road, moving.

TENTH HOUSE/ELEVENTH HOUSE COUPLE

Your Karmic Path: Your friends and the groups to which you belong are highlighted in your partnership. These people somehow help you attain your career goals and life ambitions. You both gain through the company that you keep.

Strength: It reads like a fortune cookie: Your blessings in career and with friends are many.

Challenge: Your friends may interfere with your partnership.

ELEVENTH HOUSE/TWELFTH HOUSE COUPLE

Your Karmic Path: This path could be difficult. One partner is social, the other reclusive. However, if both partners are self-aware and understand the importance of introspection, then the two energies can be merged in constructive ways, perhaps through metaphysical or spiritual exploration.

Strength: You balance each other.

Challenge: The social partner may be too social and the reclusive partner too reclusive.

TWELFTH HOUSE/FIRST HOUSE

Your Karmic Path: You draw on each other's strengths, support, and intuitive wisdom to achieve your collective dreams. Together, you may explore divination systems, cosmic mysteries, hypnosis, past-life regression, alternative healing techniques, or other areas that are out of the mainstream.

Strength: You're equal partners on this strange journey and are together because you each have strengths and insights to offer the other.

Challenge: Karmic ties and issues must be explored and, unless you both rise to the occasion, your potential won't be realized.

BEST FRIENDS

TWO SIGNS APART

W alk out into your neighborhood some evening and study the house that is two doors away from yours on either side. Unless you live in an area governed by a strict building code, where all the houses must look the same, then chances are the house two doors away differs from yours. It may be larger or smaller, have more property or windows, or be older or newer. But because the houses are located in such close proximity, they probably are compatible and complement each other. That's what this aspect is about.

A sign that is two away from yours—at an angle of 60 degrees—is called a sextile. It's considered to be an aspect of ease. Signs that are sextile don't have the same element or quality, but the elements are compatible—fire and air (Aries/Gemini) or water and earth (Taurus/Cancer). A sextile relationship may not be a wildly passionate affair that sweeps you away or that makes the ground quake. But at the heart of it, you and your partner genuinely like each other, have a strong intuitive connection, and may be each other's closest friends.

Of the possible combinations, one of the most challenging is between Virgo and Scorpio. While I'm sure there are numerous Virgos and Scorpios in partnerships that work incredibly well, this combination may not run as smoothly as the others. The major issue seems to be power—who has it, who doesn't, and how the one with the power wields it. Part of the problem may have to do with the rulership of the respective signs. Virgo is ruled by Mercury, which governs communication and the conscious mind, and Scorpio is ruled by heavy-hitter Pluto, god of the underworld, and coruled by Mars, symbol of physical and sexual energy.

Power issues crop up in any relationship that involves Scorpio, but some signs are better equipped to deal with it. Capricorn, the other sign that is sextile to Scorpio, does much better in this combination. Perhaps it's because Capricorn is ruled by Saturn, the planet that governs the rules of physical reality, and has more stamina in the face of almighty transformative Pluto.

Some of the more interesting sextile partnerships include Jimmy and Rosalyn Carter (Libra and Leo), Jack and Jackie Kennedy (Gemini and Leo), Abraham and Mary Todd Lincoln (Aquarius and Sagittarius), and Robert and Elizabeth Barrett Browning (Taurus and Pisces).

Sun Sign Combinations

This section describes how you and your partner relate to each other.

♈♊

ARIES/GEMINI COUPLE

When these two come together in a romantic relationship, the electricity is palpable. Both signs are impulsive and don't have any problem communicating what they think and feel, when they think and feel it. Neither one likes to be tied down, so this partnership has a lot of built-in latitude for both individuals. However, there's a caveat: Both signs can be jealous, but for different reasons.

Aries is taken in by the quickness of Gemini's mind, and Gemini admires Aries's capacity for dynamic action. Both signs have abundant physical energy and are able to get by on little sleep, burning their candles at both ends, but only for a limited period of time. Then they either crash and burn or crawl into bed and sleep for two days.

Aries is as direct about his or her sexuality as about everything else. Gemini is direct when it suits his or her purposes. Yet, the romance holds surprises and considerable intensity. Aries understands that Gemini must be seduced through the mind, and Gemini understands that the Aries ego must be stroked. These details aside, they genuinely enjoy each other's company in and out of bed.

Challenges? There aren't as many as there are with some of the other combinations. For an in-depth look, it's smart to compare the full birth charts for both individuals. But in a general sense, the potentially troubling areas revolve around personality quirks. Aries tends to be more physically athletic than Gemini, but Gemini is more mentally athletic. It may not seem like a big deal, but when Aries wants to go running, Gemini may be racing toward the end of a novel. Or when Gemini is rushing off to a class, Aries may be stuffing clothes in a backpack for some spur of the moment adventure.

Overall, these two feed each other's personalities and, they tend to be supportive and affectionate when it comes to romance.

♉ ♋

TAURUS/CANCER COUPLE

A bull and a crab. You wouldn't think they would get along. But this is an earth and a water combination, each of whom is a bit quirky, but with the sort of quirks the other can understand most of the time.

The qualities they have in common are impressive. Both enjoy cooking, have adventurous palates, and are security-conscious. Both enjoy their homes, property, gardens, art, books, and beautiful things. Lunar-ruled Cancer tends to be much moodier than Taurus is, but the bull compensates with stubbornness. Just like the crab that symbolizes the sign, Cancer avoids confrontation by sidling to the left or right and taking refuge in his shell. Taurus also avoids confrontation by moving into silence. Emotional explosions are pretty rare with this combination, unless one or both partners feel cornered. Then the bull rushes and the crab fights.

Quite often with this combination, there will be nodal, Moon, or Ascendant connections that indicate a karmic relationship. Compare the full birth charts of both individuals for a more complete picture of the partnership.

Cancer and Taurus are both intuitive and pick up on each other's moods, thoughts, and feelings. Cancer is also empathic and can pick up on Taurus's emotions by feeling what the bull feels—not just emotions, but also little aches, pains, and petty physical annoyances. In turn, Taurus can tune in to Cancer's crazy lunar moods and even anticipate them and take measures beforehand to mitigate them.

Drawbacks? There aren't many. Cancer can be quite jealous, and Taurus, when pushed, has quite a temper. Both are tenacious in their own ways and, once they love each other, they don't surrender the relationship easily.

$$♊ ♌$$

GEMINI/LEO COUPLE

Remember the lion in the *Wizard of Oz?* He wanted courage and hoped that the wizard would give it to him. Well, for Leo, that wizard could be Gemini, who intuitively understands the Leo need for acceptance. After all, two people live inside the Gemini skin, and the twins are always crying out to each other for acceptance. Maybe it's not the same thing, but it's close enough. These two recognize certain qualities in each other and when this relationship begins in friendship, it's more likely to survive the endless antics of the Leo ego and the Gemini duality.

One of the reasons this relationship works is because Gemini usually isn't interested in upstaging a Leo. Gemini would rather stand at the sidelines, observing, collecting facts, and taking notes. Gemini would rather blend in. And that, of course, suits Leo, who must always grab the limelight when the opportunity presents itself. Yet, Jack and Jackie Kennedy seemed to be an exception. He was the Gemini; she was the Leo. One can argue, though, that despite the fact that Jack was president, Jackie was the focal point. Her clothes. Her hair. Her famous sunglasses. Her leonine grace and dignity.

The challenges in this combination lie in the qualities of the signs. Leo is a fixed sign, as stubborn as a Taurus or a Scorpio, and Gemini is mutable, as changeable as a Sagittarius or a Pisces. Nothing drives a Leo nuttier than a partner who can't make up his or her mind or whose opinions change with the direction of the wind. If Gemini is a friend tonight and a lover tomorrow night, then what will Gemini be on the third night?

No telling. Even Gemini doesn't know.

♋♍
CANCER/VIRGO COUPLE

When I think of these two together, moonlit beaches come to mind. Cancer's head is turned toward the water, where the reflection of the Moon against the vast surface of ocean is nothing short of miraculous. Virgo's eyes are cast downward, observing the way shadows eddy and shift across the sands. Virgo notices the tiny pocks in the wet sand that clams leave as they dig in for the night; Cancer sees a pair of dolphins breaking through the surface of the water. Yet, both are experiencing harmony. Never mind that their versions of harmony differ somewhat. One way or another, they'll reach the same place within themselves and within each other.

Few people understand this relationship, but that's fine with Cancer and Virgo. They understand it. When Cancer is all moody and sullen, Virgo instinctively knows how to soothe and comfort until the mood has passed. When Virgo gets caught up in the quest for perfection, Cancer nods and agrees and cooks Virgo a terrific meal or brings out the airplane tickets that were supposed to be a birthday present. "We're going to Athens," Cancer announces, and immediately Virgo frowns. "Can we afford it?" she wonders.

Of course they can. These two are workers. Virgo is always proud of a job well done and won't give up until the job is done to the utmost perfection. Cancer works to accrue whatever he or she perceives as security. Either method ensures a happy employer.

Problems? Challenges? Well, it's a fine point, but worth noting. Cancer can be clingy, needy, or whiny. Virgo can be cuttingly critical. Catch these two on a day when they're both in their negative modes, and it's not a pretty picture.

The bottom line with these two is that they really are best friends.

♌♎
LEO/LIBRA COUPLE

Air and fire, fixed and cardinal, the lion and the…scales? What kind of scales? Who decided on scales as a symbol? And what, exactly, does that symbol mean?

That's Libra talking. Libra will debate and question just about any topic. When Libra sees an opportunity for choice, the need for balance kicks in and Libra is off and running. Leo may find this annoying at times, particularly when the lion issues his or her opinion or belief on something. Leo may think, "I'm the king, I'm right…so why are you questioning me about this? Why are you insisting on a debate?"

Libra, like Gemini and Aquarius, is a sign that entails ideas, discussion, and communication. It's the most social of the air signs, a quality that pleases Leo no end because Libra always galvanizes the troops, brings the audience into the theater, and gets the message out there. If you're a Leo politician, you want at least one Libra on your staff, preferably in a public relations position. If you're a Leo in a partnership with a Libra, then you had better bone up on your language and debating skills. You'll need them. Then again, maybe you've learned that when Libra finally makes up his or her mind it's a done deal.

But that's the crux of it for a Libra: the decision. It's tough to make a definitive decision about anything when you can see all sides of an issue. It's also tough to say no to anyone, especially to a Leo partner who expects his or her word to become law. Libra wants to keep the peace. Leo just wants to be obeyed.

So what's the attraction? That nothing is what you think it's going to be.

♍♏
VIRGO/SCORPIO COUPLE

Best friends is probably the best place to keep this relationship. Even though signs that are sextile to each other generally make great romantic partnerships, this combination may be an exception. And it has more to do with the nature of Scorpio than anything else.

I don't mean to dump on Scorpio here. I have a Scorpio Ascendant and have known my share of Scorpio Sun signs. But unless your partner is a self-aware, evolved Scorpio, then gentle Virgo with the dry wit, the cutting criticisms, the eye for detail, may be completely overwhelmed. Scorpio relationships are all too often about power. Even fellow water signs—Pisces and Cancer—should think twice before getting involved with a Scorpio. And yet, Capricorn—another sextile relationship—seems to do pretty well in a partnership with Scorpio. But more on that in the Scorpio/Capricorn section.

First, let's look at the areas that Virgo and Scorpio have in common. Their elements are compatible: earth and water. Both enjoy solitude—not necessarily as a steady diet, but they enjoy their own company. Scorpio's need to get to the bottom of everything goes along well with Virgo's penchant for details. After all, you need details to understand the bottom line. You need facts, a discriminating intellect. They often find a strange peace in each other's presence, almost as if they were communicating telepathically while the rest of the world is jammed in ultrafast chatter. And as long as the power struggles don't enter the picture, they get along fine.

When power issues surface, though, then all of Virgo's self-effacing qualities leap into the picture and things go rapidly downhill from there.

♎ ↗
LIBRA/SAGITTARIUS COUPLE

These two signs are ruled by the most expansive and fortunate planets in astrology—Venus and Jupiter. So it's no wonder Libra and Sagittarius get along so well. Both are optimistic people, the sort for whom a day is always partly sunny and a glass is always half full. Both are talkers—Libra will debate just about anything and Sagittarius seizes every opportunity to philosophize. Both enjoy socializing, having fun, and networking, and they excel when they have a "mission."

For Sadge, this mission may be spiritual or religious. In their search for the larger picture, Sagittarians often flirt with organized religion; if they move beyond that, they eventually create a spirituality and a worldview that is uniquely their own. Libras may also get involved with spiritual issues, but their path may be somewhat more focused. A Libra, for instance, may tackle a single fact of spiritual thought, such as reincarnation or life after death. Both signs seek to realize ideals.

These two usually find all the mental and physical stimulation in each other that any couple could want. Both signs, however, may have problems with commitment. Sadge may view a commitment as tantamount to prison, and Libra may see it as an end to his or her pursuit of ideals. Libra may get fed up with Sadge's proselytizing, particularly with religious types. But Sadge is just as likely to become annoyed with Libra's endless debates about everything from what kind of toothpaste to buy to what kind of dog to rescue from the pound. Once these two move past these minor bumps, however, they can accomplish just about anything together.

♏ ♑
SCORPIO/CAPRICORN COUPLE

Secretive, elusive, enigmatic: All these adjectives fit Scorpio, but none reveals the full picture. Even under the best of circumstances, Scorpio is tough to understand. Then again, so is Capricorn.

Both signs understand what power is and, in their individual ways, aspire to achieve it. With Capricorn, the achievement tends to be in terms of career; for Scorpio, it's the absolute bottom line. So when these two signs combine energies in a romantic partnership (or any kind of partnership), there's no stopping them. Neither sign is a quitter. They will achieve what they set out to achieve. And perhaps their mutual perception of power is what makes them such compatible partners.

Scorpio's tendency toward secrecy probably won't bother Capricorn. The goat understands that we all have secrets and really just isn't interested. You won't find a Capricorn going through a partner's private letters and journals, but suspicious Scorpio might do it, looking for evidence of…well, something. Capricorn won't ever pry into Scorpio's past, won't prod with questions and curiosities, but instead accepts Scorpio just as he or she is. Scorpio's ability to take so much on faith may puzzle

Capricorn at times, but this—like so many other things about Scorpio—is just business as usual.

They get along well in bed. Blunt, but there you have it. Sex for these two can be a transcendental experience. And once they've committed to the relationship, they usually are loyal to each other as well.

So where're the challenges in this combination? Perhaps the major challenge has to do with money. For Scorpio, money is power; Capricorn simply doesn't want to be without it. Where Scorpio fears exposure of his or her innermost secrets, Capricorn fears poverty. The differences are subtle but important.

SAGITTARIUS/AQUARIUS COUPLE

Here's another fire and air combination, and the electrical connections between these two are sure to baffle the rest of us—but neither one cares what the rest of us think.

Both are independent, but in different ways. Sadge insists on being free to get up and go at a moment's notice, and Aquarius insists on being free to pursue whatever, whenever, and however he or she chooses. One is motivated by the illusion of physical freedom and the other by the illusion of mental freedom. One is looking for the cosmic truth; the other is looking for whatever is genuine.

Uranus-ruled Aquarius hates pretense, and in that respect, has a true soul mate in Sagittarius. Aquarius doesn't mind Sadge's bluntness, either, and would rather deal with raw honesty than hours of convoluted conversation from a water sign. Of course, Aquarius loves his fellow air signs almost as much as he loves his own sign. Air signs speak a language that Aquarius understands instantly; with fire signs, it takes a bit of patience to get all the subtleties and nuances.

Sadge, an idealist and a seeker, and Aquarius, a humanitarian who honors the spark of individuality in all people, are perfectly suited for each other as long as the relationship doesn't veer anywhere close to dogma. And this is precisely where things can go very wrong.

If Sadge gets on his high horse about the truth, the way, and the light, Aquarius will be gone in a flash. The water bearer, a fixed sign, will not be preached to, converted, or suckered into anything that smacks of spiritual dogma. Sagittarius, ever the adventurer, will bow out when Aquarius heads into the realm of the very strange.

Other than that, this relationship has enough variety to keep both parties interested for a very long time, even if they never officially tie the knot.

♑♓

CAPRICORN/PISCES COUPLE

They come together as the best of friends, comrades who understand where the other is coming from and where the other is headed. No small task. Capricorn is ruled by almighty Saturn and Pisces, by ethereal Neptune, show do these two manage to get to a place that's mutually acceptable?

Ask Pisces, who understands that water assumes the shape of the vessel into which it's poured. So let's look at this combination in light of vessels and shapes. Capricorn, by her very nature, forces Pisces to become more practical, grounded, and less abstract. But Pisces, by his very nature, forces Capricorn to stretch in terms of imagination and possibilities. In real life, it works something like this:

Pisces: "My favorite movie is *Dead Again*."
Capricorn: "The one about reincarnation?"
Pisces: "Right."
Capricorn: "Please tell me you're kidding."
Pisces: "Okay, I'm kidding."
Capricorn: "You aren't kidding. You believe in that stuff. I like Emma Thompson, but c'mon, there's no proof."
Pisces: "I have proof. I knew you in Atlantis."
Capricorn (rolling the eyes, smirking): "Yeah? And what was that life about?"
And Pisces tells Capricorn exactly what that life was about, and somewhere deep inside the goat, belief systems begin to shift, windows of

perception crack open. Capricorn is awed by the Piscean ability to plunge into intuitive and clairvoyant depths, and this is one area where they differ greatly. The goat is a creature of the land and the fish is a creature of the sea. Even though the elements complement each other, there are places Capricorn simply can't follow when Pisces leads—and vice versa. But as long as they understand that about each other and respect each other's differences, problems between these two should be minimal.

Possible challenges? That Capricorn will control Pisces because the fish is too willing to bend and give in to make the relationship work. Then Pisces may seek escapism through drugs, alcohol, or sex with someone other than his or her partner.

AQUARIUS/ARIES COUPLE

Excitement is the name of this air/fire combination. Uranus-ruled Aquarius and Mars-ruled Aries have more in common than they know, and foremost among these qualities is a spirit that enjoys exploration. No matter what they're exploring—a place, an idea, a new restaurant—they get swept up in the moment and squeeze it for everything it's worth.

Both signs are idiosyncratic and that often becomes a bond between them. They instinctively understand each other's quirks. Aries doesn't care what other people think of him or his partner and Aquarius, of course, never gives it a second thought. The Aquarian mind, that lightning-quick perception that usually sees the much broader implications of every action, intrigues Aries. And Aquarius is fascinated by the ram's ability to make snap decisions. Aquarius, a fixed sign, is apt to mull things over, to project the path of a particular decision into the future. Aries acts on instinct and doesn't worry about tomorrow.

And this is one area where Aquarius and Aries may get into trouble. Even though the water bearer is given to erratic and quirky behavior, he or she is more practical than Aries when it comes to money—earning and spending it and stashing some away for the future. But if Aries entrusts the finances to Aquarius and Aquarius entrusts adventure to Aries, then the only other potential problem is the Aries ego.

For an Aries, much of life is about himself: "My love life, my vacation, my way of doing things, me me me." So many of the ram's decision are made on the spur of the moment that there isn't time to consider anyone else. This may become an irritant even to the most patient and humanitarian Aquarius and is something Aries needs to be aware of even in the best of relationships.

♓♉
PISCES/TAURUS COUPLE

Pisces is symbolized by two fish swimming in opposite directions. Like Gemini, it's considered to be a sign of duality. Even though the duality won't be as obvious as it is with the twins, there are times when three people are involved in this partnership.

Taurus is the practical one in this partnership. This suits Pisces, who is delighted to have someone else mind the finances, do the gardening, and even take over the cooking. In return, Pisces will do what Pisces does best—imagine, intuit, create, heal, empathize. And in between, Pisces will add color, pizzazz, and comfort to the bull's life.

As in any relationship with Pisces, there undoubtedly is a strong karmic tie between these two partners. Taurus will sense it just as readily as Pisces does. Although Pisces will accept the validity of such feelings on faith, Taurus may have to mull it all over for a while. But once the bull recognizes the truth of the situation, acceptance quickly follows.

Taurus has a deeply mystical nature that is connected to the Earth, nature, and the seasons. The mystical nature of Pisces is more fluid and tougher to pin down. But because these two signs are an earth and water combination, the slight differences in how they approach spirituality and metaphysics is complementary. They learn from each other.

Possible challenges? When Taurus needs or wants an answer, Pisces may not be willing to provide one. The fish is slippery and elusive and refuses to be pinned down even on the simplest things, much less something as complex as an emotion. Also, the legendary stubbornness of the bull could be a potential problem for these two. But overall, there are few impediments to a mutually enjoyable and loving relationship.

Sun/North Node Connections

T he descriptions below address both variations of a combination. If you have a first house Sun and your partner's North Node falls in your third house or if your Sun is in the third house and your partner's North Node falls in your first house, then the first description applies to both.

The Sun/North Node connections describe your path as a couple—the strengths and challenges you face in the relationship and how you and your partner evolve through the partnership to achieve your individual potentials. However, you can apply the descriptions to anyone in your life.

When astrologers compare a couple's chart, they often use a biwheel, with one partner's chart in the inner wheel and the other person's chart in the outer wheel, as you did in the practice section at the beginning of part two. This enables you to see where your partner's planets fall in your houses and which of your planets are hit. The ways in which your partner's planets impact yours describe what your partner brings to the relationship. When your partner's chart is in the inner wheel and yours is in the biwheel, it indicates what you bring to your partner in the relationship. Always start with your natal Sun, which is the basic archetype of who you are.

By now, you've either downloaded your and your partner's charts from the Internet or have used one of the blank charts in the back of the book to place your Sun and North Node and those of your partner in the appropriate houses. So read on!

FIRST HOUSE/THIRD HOUSE COUPLE

Your Karmic Path: Through self-expression and communication skills, you and your partner bolster and support each other's goals and self-confidence. You encourage each other to develop natural talents and abilities. In this way, one of you can break free from the deeply engrained belief that the needs of others must be placed before the needs of the self. This doesn't imply selfishness, merely a need for independent thought.

Strength: At the heart of it, your close friendship is your comfort zone, your bulwark against the world.

Challenge: One of you occasionally gets caught up in opinionated bragging.

SECOND HOUSE/FOURTH HOUSE COUPLE

Your Karmic Path: You define your values in the partnership and apply them to your home life. Part of this path involves achieving financial prosperity—not for the sake of materialism, but to learn how to apply spiritual values to finances and to use spiritual truths to manifest prosperity.

Strength: Your home life is one of the greatest opportunities for spiritual and personal growth.

Challenge: Conflict between home and domestic obligations may be a challenge.

THIRD HOUSE/FIFTH HOUSE COUPLE

Your Karmic Path: Creativity and communication are major themes in your partnership. You may combine energies to work on a creative project together that could involve children (your own or those of other people), teaching, writing, public speaking, music, or the arts. You absorb and share knowledge and information that somehow furthers the spiritual path of the relationship every bit as much as it furthers your individual spiritual paths.

Strength: Creative brainstorming and the capacity to dream are important to both of you. Use them to achieve whatever you set out to do together.

Challenge: You'll need to find a way to manifest your creative abilities without getting distracted.

FOURTH HOUSE/SIXTH HOUSE COUPLE

Your Karmic Path: Your home life provides a sound and stable foundation for your daily work life and for your health. You and your partner may be particularly health conscious and diligent in your selection of foods, diet, and exercise. You may explore the role of belief systems and their impact on health and on how your deepest beliefs help create your daily reality.

Strength: Your self-expression focuses on the home and on creating stability within the home.

Challenge: You have a need for recognition in your work. Don't allow that need to become obsessive.

FIFTH HOUSE/SEVENTH HOUSE COUPLE

Your Karmic Path: You've come together in this life to explore a creative partnership. How you define this as a couple is entirely up to you, as long as you are mutually cooperative without thinking about personal gain. If you help each other with an eye on personal gain, you'll lose. And this isn't something that you can pretend. It has to be genuine, right from the heart, or it doesn't count!

Strength: Your best achievements may come through your work with your partner.

Challenge: Friends or social acquaintances may interfere in your partnership. Be cautious about selfishness in this partnership: It could be your undoing.

SIXTH HOUSE/EIGHTH HOUSE COUPLE

Your Karmic Path: Your path is to explore cooperative teamwork with your partner in the areas of daily work and joint resources. By learning that you can depend on each other in your daily work lives, a bond of trust is built up that allows each of you to explore esoteric topics, such as reincarnation, life after death, and the role your deeper beliefs play in your lives.

Strength: By combining resources, your opportunities for financial prosperity are greater. Together, you learn the role of free will in the larger picture of your lives.

Challenge: One of you is tempted to rely on your partner to make financial and work decisions.

SEVENTH HOUSE/NINTH HOUSE COUPLE

Your Karmic Path: Through your partnership, your individual worldview, spirituality, and grasp on broader philosophical issues is broadened. This is the configuration in the Nancy Reagan example. Through her marriage, Nancy Reagan became the "power behind the throne" of the presidency. Nancy Reagan's Cancer Sun sign is just one degree away from the 13-degree Cancer Sun of the U.S. Its placement in the ninth house is somehow appropriate, because this house governs politics.

Strength: You have a clear understanding of the dynamics of your relationship and work well together as a team.

Challenge: Power is your greatest challenge.

EIGHTH HOUSE/TENTH HOUSE COUPLE

Your Karmic Path: Your partnership is about sharing your resources to achieve professional ambitions and desires. Together, you learn the roles freewill and spiritual beliefs play in manifesting career opportunities. One of you may be interested in spiritual or metaphysical topics and this interest influences your partnership in a positive way.

Strength: It's a joint effort and you both fully realize it.

Challenge: You need to rid yourselves of old attitudes pertaining to money and career.

NINTH HOUSE/ELEVENTH HOUSE COUPLE

Your Karmic Path: Through your group associations and networks of friends and acquaintances, you and your partner achieve a greater understanding of metaphysics and the higher mind. Foreign countries and cultures, higher education, publishing, and politics also play into this picture. Your personal creative goals are achieved with the support of friends.

Strength: The spiritual evolution of the partnership benefits both of you individually. Through each other, you learn how to manifest your desires.

Challenge: Your challenge is in releasing outdated thought patterns that hold you back.

TENTH HOUSE/TWELFTH HOUSE COUPLE

Your Karmic Path: One of you gains through anything that occurs behind the scenes, and the other gains through everything that's public. This dichotomy can be resolved within the parameters of the relationship, but at times it may have a karmic feel to it that's uncomfortable. Sometimes, this combination can bring about great psychic development within both individuals.

Strength: As partners, you're protected from people who work against you.

Challenge: The partner behind the scenes may feel cheated.

ELEVENTH HOUSE/FIRST HOUSE COUPLE

Your Karmic Path: You need to learn independence from others without severing your friendships and group associations. It's through your friends and networks that you learn what is most important to each of you as individuals and as partners.

Strength: You value the partnership without sacrificing your individual needs.

Challenge: Asserting your individual needs may cause conflict.

TWELFTH HOUSE/SECOND HOUSE COUPLE

Your Karmic Path: A lot of your combined energy goes into earning money and defining your personal values. You both may be more interested in solitude and your inner lives than in having numerous friends and an active social life.

Strength: Through the partnership, you have the opportunity to develop your individual creative talents.

Challenge: Your solitude can make you virtual recluses.

TEACHER

THREE SIGNS APART

Think of the people in your life—family, friends, lovers, mentors—whose Sun signs are three removed from yours. Your signs share the same quality—cardinal, mutable, or fixed—but have different and incompatible elements. This aspect is called a square; the signs are ninety degrees apart.

Check the table on the following page.

TABLE 5: **SQUARES**

Your Sun Sign	Square to
♈ Aries	Cancer, Capricorn
♉ Taurus	Leo, Aquarius
♊ Gemini	Virgo, Pisces
♋ Cancer	Aries, Libra
♌ Leo	Taurus, Scorpio
♍ Virgo	Gemini, Sagittarius
♎ Libra	Capricorn, Cancer
♏ Scorpio	Leo, Aquarius
♐ Sagittarius	Virgo, Pisces
♑ Capricorn	Libra, Aries
♒ Aquarius	Scorpio, Taurus
♓ Pisces	Gemini, Sagittarius

What roles have individuals played in your life whose Sun signs are square to yours? How do you perceive them? How do you think they perceive you?

It's likely that your relationship has a teacher/student texture to it. But unlike traditional relationships of this sort, you exchange roles constantly. Sometimes you're the teacher and the other person is the student, and vice versa. You may find that of the two signs that are square to yours, you know more people of one sign than the other.

As a Gemini, both Pisces and Virgo are square to my sign. Of the two, Virgo individuals are a constant theme in my life. My daughter is a double Virgo—Sun and Moon. My closest writer friend is a Virgo. My agent is a Virgo. I've had a number of Virgo editors. If I dig a little deeper and include the signs of other people's Moon, Ascendant, Venus, and Mars, the picture gets even stranger. My husband has a Virgo Moon. My father has a Virgo Ascendant. I could go on, but you get the idea here. I apparently have much to learn from Virgos, or they from me, or both.

If you find a recurring pattern with any sign, but particularly with one that is three removed from your own, pay attention. It means that the relationship holds great potential for learning and growth. In a romantic relationship, the same potential is there, but because the emotions have a different quality, the square can be challenging—not impossible, just challenging.

When I was researching possible examples for this chapter, I realized I had an excellent example in my own family. My mother was a Capricorn, my father is a Libra. The theme of teacher was prevalent in their fifty-six years together, but in ways neither of them expected when they met in 1942. The world, of course, was a vastly different place then—maybe even a different universe, when you think about it—and the culture in which my parents came of age undoubtedly influenced their relationship. But in astrology, a square is a square, a challenging aspect regardless of the century into which you're born.

A square generates tension but galvanizes you and your partner into action. It seems to create obstacles or challenges, unless you learn to focus less on your differences and more on the ways in which you're compatible. Squares in a relationship aren't meant to feel comfortable; but with self-realized individuals, the square is a call both to learn and to teach, with partners exchanging roles as the situation and natural flow of events call for it.

As cardinal signs, my parents used energy in the same focused, directed way. My dad, a late Libra, concentrated his energy on his career and on his family; my mother, an early Capricorn, focused her energy on her family and friends. From my mother, my father learned to expand his social network and friendships and grew to enjoy animals as much as she did. From my father, my mother learned to embrace foreign cultures and people and worldviews vastly different from her own. From him, she learned how to relax into the moment.

From an astrological point of view, their Sun sign roles sometimes seemed reversed to me. My Libra father should have been the more social of the two, but that seemed to be my mother's domain, perhaps due to her gregarious Sagittarius Moon rather than her Capricorn Sun. My Capricorn mother was supposed to be the more professionally ambitious of the two, but her ambitions were for my father and my sister and me. True to the Capricorn Sun, she enjoyed possessions—not in a gross materialistic sense, but because, I suspect, they gave her a sense of place, of roots. She collected figurines and glassware from her travels and my father, true to the Libra Sun, enjoyed art and music. They helped broaden each other's perspective on beauty.

I never heard them argue. This isn't surprising; Capricorn and Libra dislike confrontation and messy emotional entanglements. Their disagreements tended to be about large issues. My dad claims he hadn't given much thought to having children, but my mother wanted kids and she won on that score. When the political situation in Venezuela, where we lived at the time, began to deteriorate, my dad decided to take early retirement and move back to the U.S. My mother wanted to return to Oklahoma, where she'd grown up, where her mother and siblings lived. But my dad associated Oklahoma with poverty and the depression and saw Florida as a place rich with promise. So they moved to Florida. Besides, as he pointed out, Florida has great weather!

It seems that within the context of their relationship, they learned when to capitulate and when to stand firm, when to assume the role of teacher and when to assume the role of student. And maybe that's the real secret of successfully navigating the "teacher" relationship.

Sun Sign Combinations

This section describes how you and your partner relate to each other.

♈ ♋

ARIES/CANCER COUPLE

Yes, there are times when this relationship hurts. It's inevitable when you mix a fire sign with a water sign. Aries, the fire, learns and navigates life through dynamic action; Cancer, the water, learns and navigates life through emotion. Aries, so often impatient and blunt, says something that offends Cancer or hurts the crab's feelings. So Cancer skitters off into his shell to hide and sulk for a while. Or Cancer's moodiness shuts Aries out, which is hurtful to Aries.

But there are also times when this relationship is exciting, stimulating, passionate, and adventurous, and it's these times you should strive to remember.

From the ram, Cancer learns how to pursue what she loves, to not give up or surrender in the face of challenge. The crab sees Aries literally ramming his way through obstacles and begins to understand that sometimes, life must be hit head on, confronted, seized. From the crab, Aries learns that some challenges must be met by molding yourself to the situation, by going with the flow and moving as water moves, around an obstacle.

Cancer is sensitive to minute fluctuations in emotions and can read Aries extremely well without a word being spoken. The ram may find this occasionally disturbing, but most of the time he enjoys the telepathic connection. Aries has excellent instincts and when he focuses them on Cancer's strange and erratic moods, he grasps the underlying truths of whatever triggered the mood.

The intuitive bond between Aries and Cancer can get them through trying times, but at some point it's necessary to verbalize what they are feeling. And to verbalize it to each other. This is where problems may surface. If Cancer isn't in the mood to talk, then there won't be any discussion, period. Aries, forever short on patience, may blow up over the crab's unwillingness to talk and quickly learns that anger only drives the crab deeper into his shell.

If both partners can maintain an openness to each other's quirks and accommodate them in the relationship, then this partnership can work very well on many different levels. Sexually, it can be exhilarating. Cancer enjoys Aries's passion and Aries enjoys the way Cancer nurtures those passions. And let's face it, Aries, you love it when Cancer pampers you!

♉ ♌

TAURUS/LEO COUPLE

Whenever two fixed signs are involved with each other, the main risk in the relationship is extreme stubbornness. You both are so sure you're right that you cling to your position regardless. Or one partner tries to coerce the other partner into doing or believing something in which he or she has zero interest.

Here's another tension creator:

Leo: "How do I look in this new dress?"

Taurus (without glancing up from his book): "Fine."

Leo: "You didn't even look at me."

Taurus: "I did, too. And I'm looking now."

Leo: "Then say something."

Taurus: "You look fine."

In this scenario, Leo wants to be told she is beautiful, stunning, ravishing—not that she merely looks fine. Leo must always feel like royalty and be treated like royalty by her partner. Even if Taurus reveres

Leo, the lion shouldn't expect a steady stream of accolades from the bull. It just isn't the Taurean way.

Conversely, Taurus needs loyalty and affection from Leo so that he knows he's appreciated and loved. But Leo is often so wrapped up in herself that she isn't fully present when she's with the bull. Taurus is offended and hurt by this, even though it's rarely intentional on Leo's part.

However, if all of this can be dealt with honestly, with each partner verbalizing what he or she needs, then the relationship holds great potential for mutual growth. From Taurus, Leo learns the value of stability, loyalty, and emotional dependability. Leo learns that beauty, art, and music don't have to be flashy and loud, with lots of pomp and circumstance to be good. The lion's artistic values are enlarged and broadened in this relationship.

From Leo, Taurus learns that self-confidence produces results and that sometimes you simply have to get out there and sell yourself and your product with such fire and enthusiasm that the buyer simply can't resist.

Sexually and romantically, though, these two should get along well. Taurus's sensuality and Leo's passion blend nicely in bed.

♊♍
GEMINI/VIRGO COUPLE

The chemistry between Gemini and Virgo is primarily mental. Gemini appreciates Virgo's exquisite precision with details; Virgo admires Gemini's versatility. Both signs are ruled by Mercury, the planet of communication, so regardless of how challenging this partnership may be at times, you can always talk about it.

This partnership lends itself to a constant and lively exchange of ideas and information. Gemini collects information in a restless search for how everything in life fits together, and Virgo gathers information as part of his quest for unity. Gemini asks: "*How* does this work?" Virgo asks: "*Why* does this work?" And then Virgo takes it apart, scrutinizes it, and puts it back together again. Their approaches to the question differ, but they often arrive at the same place.

Problems surface for several reasons. Gemini generally isn't concerned about perfection, but perfection is paramount for Virgo. As a result, Virgo can be quite self-deprecating ("I'm not good enough, cute enough, smart enough") or turns that critical eye on his partner.

Virgo: "That bed was made in a sloppy way, you know."

Gemini: "So if you don't like it, do it yourself."

Virgo: "We agreed that making the bed would be your chore."

Gemini: "Hey, give me a break. I just got up five minutes ago."

Virgo should never forget that he lives with two people—the sunny Gemini and the other Gemini. The dichotomy between these two personalities can disturb Virgo, who often isn't sure which twin is in charge on a given day. Virgo tends to be more serious than Gemini and is puzzled when the twins snap at one moment, then laugh at the next.

Quirks and tensions aside, though, there's tremendous potential for growth in this partnership, particularly in a creative area. If Gemini and Virgo collaborate creatively, the results may surprise both of them!

From Virgo, Gemini learns to be more attentive to details and precision. Through example, Virgo teaches Gemini how to be more discerning and how to take a deeper look at the inner workings of things, such as relationships, motives, oracles, the cosmos; nothing is too large or too small. From Gemini, Virgo learns that no topic is forbidden and every question can be asked. Gemini also teaches Virgo how to lighten up and have fun!

♋ ♎
CANCER/LIBRA COUPLE

Because Cancer is ruled by the Moon and Libra is ruled by Venus, there can be great softness between these two if they can move beyond their differences and learn from each other.

Okay, the differences. At times, both partners will feel as if they're involved with an alien. Libra puzzles over Cancer's moody silences; Cancer is mystified by Libra's constant need to be fair, just, and balanced. Libra is astonished at how intuitive and perceptive Cancer is (but enjoys it!), and Cancer is astonished at how Libra can talk to anyone, anywhere, at any time (but also loves that quality!). The primary disparity between these two is that they filter their experiences in different ways: Cancer through emotions and intuition and Libra through the mind and social instincts.

Both Cancer and Libra are cardinal signs, so they use energy in a focused, singular way. They find a path and stick to it. However, Cancer wants so much to be understood that it sometimes exhausts Libra, who tends to be a very good listener. But after listening for a very long time to the reasons for Cancer's many mood changes, Libra may get fed up and seek companionship elsewhere.

Generally, Cancer's view of the world is far more subjective than that of Libra, and this can lead to a lot of inner dissection that may become tedious for Libra. Cancer may get fed up with Libra's constant networking, phone conversations, parties, and social activities. "Why can't we just stay home tonight?" Cancer will moan upon hearing about a social engagement Libra simply has to keep. But the weird and wonderful part of this relationship is that both have a sense of humor and terrific imaginations. They truly are romantics. And when you love each other, these traits can go a very long way toward mitigating disagreements.

I knew a Cancer/Libra couple whose disagreements nearly always centered around his need for solitude and her need for social activities. They finally settled on a mutually agreeable arrangement by setting aside a couple of nights a week when each could indulge his or her needs with complete freedom. It sounds like a small thing, but sometimes success in relationships begins with baby steps.

From Cancer, Libra learns to look inward, to seek those beliefs that may be blocking the manifestation of a dream. From Libra, Cancer learns to look outward to friends and acquaintances who share the same beliefs. Together, these two can create something strong and lasting together, but only if they are able to move beyond their immediate needs and concerns and embrace each other's highly individualized worlds.

♌♏
LEO/SCORPIO COUPLE

Ouch. Fire and water. Bill and Hilary Clinton. This combination can be hurtful but also immensely powerful. It can be infuriating, but also loving, extremely sexual yet cold. A paradox.

Leo has a big ego; Scorpio has secrets. Leo must know that he is appreciated and loved, but Scorpio may not articulate her feelings often enough or in the right way. Leo can be arrogant and Scorpio, aloof. You can see where this is going. If you want a vivid mental picture of these two, here's one to mull over.

On the day that Bill and Hilary Clinton attended the funeral of soldiers who had been killed in the Gulf conflict, the Lewinsky scandal was brewing. I remember noticing that Hilary stood well apart from her husband and that her expression was set in granite. Her body language indicated that she was enraged and profoundly hurt. It occurred to me that the scandal wasn't just brewing for her—it had broken wide open. Within a day or two, Lewinsky's infamous dress became headline news.

A Scorpio values secrecy and privacy so deeply that to be humiliated publicly in this way is a wound the scorpion may not ever forget. Leo sees himself as a kind of royalty, so what Bill Clinton endured with impeachment hearings and Ken Starr's relentless witch hunt must have been equally humiliating. Both signs are proud, but for different reasons, and both can be extremely stubborn. It may be the stubbornness, in fact, that keeps this combination together. Neither is quick to admit defeat or failure.

On the positive side, Leo teaches Scorpio to lighten up, to have fun, to enjoy a few adventures. In turn, Scorpio teaches Leo to look within. With a Leo, Scorpio must learn to open up, to be less secretive and more upfront about what she feels. Leo must learn to draw her out, and that requires turning his attention away from himself and toward her.

Leo, ruled by the Sun, tends to be more gregarious than Scorpio, ruled by distant, powerful Pluto. The Sun symbolizes our total personality, our self-expression, and Pluto represents profound transformation. You can see how these two might get off to a bad start. But there can be a magnetic pull with this pair—a visceral, karmic attraction.

Leo is a dreamer and Scorpio must learn to honor that. Without dreams, Leo withers and dies, or leaves before he dies. However, Scorpio is insightful, intuitive, and often psychic, and Leo must learn to honor that. Not an easy task on either score. But it's not impossible, either. When these two learn how to navigate the essential mysteries of each other and join forces, then the rest of the world better watch out! When Leo and Scorpio are partners, they are a formidable team. "Us against them" becomes their mantra and pity the fools who believe otherwise.

♍ ♐
VIRGO/SAGITTARIUS COUPLE

Earth and fire. Virgo and Sagittarius are both mutable signs, so they are likely to bend over backward to accommodate each other. They communicate well, too, which always helps. But the bridge where they are most likely to meet and fare well together is in the realm of ideas.

Virgo, ruled by Mercury, loves ideas; Sagittarius, ruled by expansive, jolly Jupiter, also loves ideas. But their approaches differ vastly. Virgo dives for details, connecting the dots; Sadge immediately sweeps in for the big picture. This can create problems because while Virgo collects details, Sadge figures he already has all the answers. But when the two work together, each provides what the other lacks.

Another potentially risky area for these two is their individual approaches to money—earning it, spending it, saving it. Virgo, whom traditional wisdom identifies as the practical one in the duo, may balk at how easily and readily Sadge spends money on toys—beautiful cars and furniture, a stainless-steel fridge when a regular no-frills fridge would do just fine, thanks. However, I've known Virgos who are big spenders and Sadges who aren't. So these proclivities aren't hard and fast rules; we're all individuals and we're only talking about Sun signs.

Both signs have a sense of humor. Virgo's humor is sly, clever, and witty; Sadge's is quick, sometimes boisterous, but always funny. A couple of standup comedians, these two. And there will be plenty of times in their relationship where humor mitigates their problems. It's unlikely that either Virgo or Sadge will use his or her humor as a weapon. However, Sadge is known for his bluntness, and when he's emotionally aroused in a negative way, his sharp tongue can be extremely hurtful. "I met you when you were thin," he might say. Virgo may be shocked at the crassness, but she always recovers quickly and has a snappy comeback of her own. "When I met you, you had hair."

At their worst, Virgo nitpicks until Sadge is ready to throttle her and Sadge pontificates until Virgo is ready to tape his mouth shut. But when they find a common ground, these two can move mountains together.

♎ ♑

LIBRA/CAPRICORN COUPLE

Here's another cardinal sign combination, two leaders who are attracted to each other. In fact, in the beginning, these two may be in some sort of competition, racing neck and neck toward the finish line. Also, they are an air/earth combination and each one has a different approach to life. Because this combination is what my parents had, I can testify that when it works, it works for the long term and works well.

The caveat here is *when*.

The typical Libra is a networker, someone who loves to socialize, has numerous friends and acquaintances, and tends to define her worldview through her personal relationships. The typical Capricorn enjoys having fun and socializing, but he defines his worldview through his professional ambitions and goals. Again, there are always exceptions to this, but these traits are ripe for conflict.

However, Libra and Capricorn have a rather odd exchange going on in terms of masculine and feminine traits that actually helps their relationship. Libra, considered a masculine sign, is ruled by Venus, a feminine planet. Capricorn, considered a feminine sign, is ruled by Saturn, a masculine planet. If you think of this in Jungian terms—the anima and the animus—then it comes as no surprise that these two are able to balance each other. If Capricorn is feeling low, Libra's mood is likely to be positive and upbeat, helping Capricorn climb out of the doldrums. If Libra is feeling low, then Capricorn sweeps in with some profound philosophical observation that snaps Libra's mood into an upswing.

From Libra, Capricorn learns that all things in life—even one's ambitions—must find balance. From Capricorn, Libra learns to set and achieve definitive goals. When Capricorn is the teacher, Libra is an willing student, as long as Capricorn doesn't get too bossy. When Libra is the teacher, Capricorn makes quantum leaps in his social and networking skills.

When these two signs joins forces, when they have gotten all the petty stuff out of the way or under control, then together they can do nearly anything.

♏ ♒

SCORPIO/AQUARIUS COUPLE

Whew. Where to begin? This water/air combination is a challenge. On top of it, both are fixed signs and notoriously wedded to their own beliefs systems and lifestyles. The potential problems boil down to one very important issue: emotions. Scorpio, as a water sign, processes life through her emotions. Aquarius, an air sign, processes life through the intellect. Scorpio is emotionally intuitive and Aquarius, mentally intuitive.

Aquarius isn't an emotional sign, unless the person has a fire or water sign Moon, and that may be a problem for Scorpio. Aquarius enjoys talking through ideas, but Scorpio tends to keep things to herself, so this can be a problem for Aquarius. What's particularly intriguing about this combination is that once they work through these issues, they have much to offer—and to teach—each other.

But first, how do they navigate their differences? The best course of action is simply to allow events and emotions to unfold over time. But Scorpio can be so intensely determined to understand other people that a gradual unfolding just won't work. So Scorpio begins her subtle process of "personality divination."

Much of the time, Aquarius will be oblivious to what's really happening here. Aquarius, after all, isn't really interested in who he is; he's intrigued by ideas, possibilities, cutting-edge potentials. He'll share when he sees fit, but if he's badgered or cornered or feels that Scorpio is scrutinizing him, he'll slam the door and that will be that.

Aquarius usually doesn't place much value in personal belongings. Oh, he likes nice things—especially stuff like computers and high-tech gadgets—but he has little sense of *mine* or *yours*. Scorpio, however, is extremely conscious of what is *hers*. And when it comes down to money, it's *her* money and *your* money. Maybe separate bank accounts is the answer—at least until Scorpio learns to trust Aquarius enough to have a joint account.

You can see there are plenty of potential problem areas with these two. But what can they learn from each other?

Through Scorpio, Aquarius learns to pay closer attention to his own emotions and to ask himself why he feels (or doesn't feel) a particular emotion. He must learn to examine his inner world with the same scrutiny that he brings to the world of ideas. From Aquarius, Scorpio learns to express herself genuinely. If she's angry, she must learn to show it rather than freezing Aquarius out. Scorpio learns to be less possessive and Aquarius learns to express what he feels about his partner.

Once their powerful wills are combined, they can probably move mountains!

♐ ♓

SAGITTARIUS/PISCES COUPLE

This is another fire and water, mutable sign combination. Translated, that means: tension, energy that can be explosive, and a kind of profound puzzlement that can be either comical or tragic. Let's take a closer look.

The symbol for Sadge is a centaur, a mythological creature that is half man, half horse. The symbol for Pisces is that of two fish swimming in opposite directions. So although Pisces and Gemini are referred to as the signs of duality, Sadge has some duality, too, so it may be easier for him to understand the duality of the Piscean nature than it is for other signs. Thanks to the spiritual and mystical nature of Pisces, she can understand Sadge's need for exploring spiritual and philosophical belief systems.

Sadge is ruled by Jupiter, the jolly giant of the zodiac that expands everything it touches. Pisces is ruled by mysterious Neptune, the planet that controls mystical experiences, higher inspiration, and escapism. But Pisces is co-ruled by Jupiter, which gives these two signs something in common.

In the days when there were only seven known planets—and twelve signs—some of the planets were forced into double duty as rulers. Jupiter ended up ruling both Sagittarius and Pisces. Then when Neptune was discovered, it was assigned the rulership of mystical Pisces, a much better fit, actually, except that Neptune doesn't really tell us much about the expansiveness of the Piscean imagination. And this is where the visceral attraction happens between Pisces and Sadge.

But once the visceral attraction has come about, what do you have? It depends on the awareness each person brings to the relationship. If Pisces is on a spiritual or creative path, then the relationship is less likely to bruise and injure. If Pisces is an escapist—through booze, drugs, sex, or whatever the poison—then there will be major problems. If Sadge is at all spiritually aware, and not dogmatic about those beliefs, then the relationship could be heavenly.

Thanks to the Jupiter connection, both Pisces and Sadge are able to reach into their vast imaginations and come up with the creative equivalent of a goldmine. Both signs flourish in any relationship with strong creative bonds, and if they join forces, the results can be astonishing.

The teacher/student motif in this combination revolves around two central issues: the Sagittarian need for freedom and independence and the compassion that is so central to the Pisces nature. Pisces feels other people's pain as though it's her own and readily offers refuge and sanctuary to the injured, be it human or animal. She also has been known to be a sucker for a sob story. Sagittarius balks at how easily she trusts people and how willing she is to help complete strangers. In turn, Pisces is put off by how selfish Sadge can be at times, splitting on a moment's notice for parts unknown and too bad if he's missing a deadline or shirking responsibilities. Sadge moves with the wind.

So from Sadge, Pisces learns to be more selfish. From Pisces, Sadge learns to be more compassionate.

♑♈
CAPRICORN/ARIES COUPLE

Earth and fire typically confront challenges in a romantic relationship. The problems are rarely insurmountable, but patience and commitment are required to navigate them successfully. With Capricorn and Aries, however, the challenges are compounded by their respective rulers.

Capricorn is ruled by Saturn, the heavy of the zodiac. It keeps Capricorn grounded and generally conservative, and it explains why most

Capricorns consider life to be serious business. Aries is ruled by Mars, the fiery warrior. Blame him when Aries has a temper tantrum, leaps impulsively from one project to another (sometimes without completing the first one), and rushes headlong into relationships and situations that he should avoid. Capricorn, true to her Saturnian nature, holds back, delays, and scrutinizes all the options; Aries, true to the nature of Mars, acts instinctively or rashly. Capricorn sometimes has trouble expressing his emotions; Aries rarely has that problem.

These differences are often the very reason these two come together to begin with. Capricorn is drawn to the Aries brand of courage and conviction, and Aries is attracted to Capricorn's dilatory approach and carefully drawn strategies. Capricorn, never one to take unnecessary risks, is captivated by the risks that Aries takes almost daily. Opposites definitely attract and when they attract on a sexual, visceral level, the results can be five days straight of lovemaking. Then real life steps in, and that's where the problems start.

Aries: "You're going to work today?"

Capricorn: "I called in sick for the last three days. I have to go to work."

Aries (reaching for Capricorn's hand): "Aw, c'mon, another day won't hurt."

Capricorn: "I've got bills to pay and deadlines to meet. You should go to work, too, you know. We can't just laze around like this for the rest of our lives."

Aries: "Listen, there's this really fantastic lake and restaurant I want you to see just north of the city. Let's leave now."

Capricorn (tempted, but shaking her head): "I can't."

She walks out of the room and Aries lies there, brooding, unable to understand why she can't just forget work for another day.

This scene is magnified and complicated over the course of their relationship. Unless boundaries are drawn and parameters are set up early in the relationship, the goat and the ram won't last a season together. However, there are ways around this possibly dismal end.

Capricorn must learn to loosen up and be a bit more adventurous, and Aries must learn the value of planning. This doesn't mean that

Capricorn has to be willing to quit her job and take off on a moment's notice with nothing except a backpack. It doesn't mean that Aries must squash his spontaneity. But if each learns to give a little, to deviate somewhat from what he or she has been up to this point in life, if they both understand that they are the scriptwriters of their own lives, then there's no telling what sort of grand adventure this relationship will bring.

AQUARIUS/TAURUS COUPLE

Any time two fixed signs come together, stubbornness is one of the issues. The water bearer and the bull each has a particular way of living, thinking, and feeling, and each is convinced that his or her way is the right way. Neither of them readily admits this, but it's usually evident in their intractable opinions and arguments.

Aquarius, ruled by unpredictable Uranus, has an edgy, idiosyncratic intellect; is idealistic; loves concepts and ideas; and holds tightly to his opinions and beliefs. Taurus, ruled by the much softer Venus, is stable, grounded, and more self-contained. Her sense of touch is as finely honed as the Aquarian intellect. Taurus also holds firmly to her opinions and ideas, but if she can be convinced that Aquarius's ideas are practical (and that's not an easy thing to do), then she may be willing to step outside her box and join Aquarius in an adventure.

Taurus's sensuality is earthy, focused fully in her body and senses. Aquarius's sensuality begins in the mind. Seduce Aquarius's mind, and the rest is easy.

To navigate this combination successfully, both signs must be patient and committed to making the relationship work. They must also be willing to learn from each other, something that should be easier for these two signs than any square combination with a fire sign. From Taurus, Aquarius must learn an appreciation for physical reality—the Earth, the body, the magnificence of the senses. From Aquarius, Taurus must learn the value of ideas, technology, individuality, and eccentricity. And then they must learn to talk to each other openly and honestly about feelings.

It doesn't sound too difficult, does it?

♓♊

PISCES/GEMINI COUPLE

Two mutable signs that are square to each other probably have an easier time of making a relationship work than two fixed or two cardinal signs do. As flexible, versatile people, they seem to be more willing to go with the flow of events, to bend when one must bend, to hold firm when that's called for. Yet, this combination is water and air, two elements that aren't comfortable together, and they are ruled respectively by Neptune and Mercury, two very different planets.

Pisces dreams; Gemini flies. Pisces swim; Gemini drops through space without a parachute. Pisces is usually more intuitively tuned in to the esoteric, the strange, and the mysterious than Gemini is. But Gemini often finds an intellectual fascination with these subjects. That's a point in their favor. If they can find a common language, a common myth that unites them, then they have a chance together. Let's eavesdrop:

Pisces: "So how did you feel about that?"

Gemini: "About what?"

Pisces: "That synchronicity we had earlier today, in the car, when the turtle crossed the road."

Gemini: "Wow! You're right. We were going to watch the sea turtles lay their eggs on the beach—and a turtle crossed our path. But what does the turtle mean?"

Pisces: "That we need to slow down, to protect ourselves?"

Gemini: "Or that turtles are just…well, really beautiful creatures."

A common language has been born. But this conversation could just as easily collapse into confusion because Gemini is moving at the speed of light, too rushed to be bothered, and Pisces is drifting through the silence of her soul, deaf to everyone and everything.

Another intriguing facet of the Pisces/Gemini combination is that both are dual signs—represented by two of something—two fish and twins. This suggests abrupt moods changes and a duality in persona (as in: who am I living with *today?*). For the fish, the mood change tends to be subtle, a kind of sliding down into depression or a gradual rise into effervescence. For Gemini, the mood changes are more abrupt and mercurial. One moment Gemini is laughing, and the next moment she's weeping or shouting. So, in this combination, you actually are dealing with *four* people, *four* personalities, and that's a crowd even in a king-size bed!

Let's whittle the relationship down to just two people in that king-size bed. Pisces must learn to appreciate Gemini's mental agility, and Gemini must learn to appreciate Pisces's emotional agility. When Pisces has a gut feeling about something, Gemini must pay attention; when Gemini senses a change in the wind of their life, Pisces must pay attention. Give and take. Always.

And by the way, you two, good luck!

Sun/North Node
Connections

T he descriptions below address both variations of a combination. If you have a first house Sun and your partner's North Node falls in your fourth house, or if your Sun is in the fourth house and your partner's North Node falls in your first, then the first description applies to both.

The Sun/North Node combinations describe your path as a couple—the strengths and challenges you face in the relationship and how you and your partner evolve through the partnership to achieve your individual potentials. However, you can apply the descriptions to anyone in your life.

When astrologers compare a couple's chart, they often use a biwheel, with one partner's chart in the inner wheel and the other person's chart in the outer wheel, just as you practiced at the beginning of part two. This enables you to see where your partner's planets fall in your houses and which of your planets are hit. The ways in which your partner's planets impact yours describes what your partner brings to the relationship. When your partner's chart is in the inner wheel and yours is in the biwheel, it indicates what you bring to your partner in the relationship. Always start with your natal Sun, which is the basic archetype of who you are.

By now, you've either downloaded your and your partner's charts from the Internet or have used one of the blank charts in the back of the book to place your Sun and North Node and those of your partner in the appropriate houses. So read on!

FIRST HOUSE/FOURTH HOUSE COUPLE

Your Karmic Path: Self-expression within the context of your family/home life is where you and your partner's student/teacher relationship meets its greatest challenges—and your greatest triumphs. One of you may be more domestic or home-oriented than the other and could have parental issues that stem back to childhood. In some way, your partner helps you confront and deal with the issues, so that you can move forward spiritually and creatively in your life.

Strength: Your partnership is central to your happiness as individuals. Even though you both are independent, you're stronger as a unit.

Challenge: Domestic issues may interfere with professional goals and ambitions.

SECOND HOUSE/FIFTH HOUSE COUPLE

Your Karmic Path: As a couple, your path is defined by an exploration of your personal values through your creative drives, your children, and romance. These areas may also be where the teacher/student motif plays out. One of you has a close relationship with children or your creative ideas are leagues ahead of their time; the other is focused on money and the use of personal resources. To navigate this combination successfully may require balancing the demands of children and work. There are strong past-life ties with your children.

Strength: Your creative bond is the glue that keeps the relationship together through hard times. There could be strong past-life patterns operating in the relationship, and one of you is more aware of these patterns than the other. The teacher/student motif may be operative in this area.

Challenge: Is one of you a workaholic?

THIRD HOUSE/SIXTH HOUSE COUPLE

Your Karmic Path: Communication, siblings, neighborhood, daily work routine, and health are the themes in your relationship. Siblings, other relatives, or coworkers may help or hinder the relationship. The teacher/student motif may revolve around health or daily work issues.

Strength: You're able to communicate with each other honestly and openly, a prerequisite to any successful relationship. Past-life ties with siblings or coworkers are likely.

Challenge: One of you may put siblings or coworkers above your partner.

FOURTH HOUSE/SEVENTH HOUSE COUPLE

Your Karmic Path: Your parents or your roles as parents somehow impact your relationship with each other. The teacher/student theme revolves around parental and intimacy issues. There are strong karmic ties with your parents and with each other.

Strength: You both bring an awareness of past-life ties to your relationship. Even if you can't articulate that awareness, you feel it when you're in each other's presence. You're here, together, to resolve what was left undone in other incarnations.

Challenge: Parents may interfere in the relationship.

FIFTH HOUSE/EIGHTH HOUSE COUPLE

Your Karmic Path: Through sharing your resources and creative endeavors with others, you and your partner also teach and learn from each other. Children may be part of the creativity in your relationship. The "shared resources" part of this equation could involve banking, taxes, insurance, mortgages, or simply metaphysical knowledge. There can be a profound awareness of your past-life ties.

Strength: You are supportive of each other's creative strengths.

Challenge: The balance between pleasure/fun and the serious aspects of life is a challenge.

SIXTH HOUSE/NINTH HOUSE COUPLE

Your Karmic Path: As a couple, your daily work is bound up in some way with your worldviews, philosophies, and spiritual beliefs. These areas are also the ones in which you share a student/teacher relationship. You may be fully aware of your karmic ties.

Strength: You're committed to your spiritual beliefs.

Challenge: One of you may be a workaholic.

SEVENTH HOUSE/TENTH HOUSE COUPLE

Your Karmic Path: As partners, you seek to balance the demands of your relationship and your respective careers. Your karmic ties are likely to surface again and again as part of the conflict between your careers and your relationship until you resolve the issue as a couple. The balance issue is where your student/teacher relationship will occur.

Strength: An inner awareness of the true dynamics of the relationship is your greatest strength. In terms of impacting the larger world, you're stronger as a couple.

Challenge: Selfishness may be your biggest challenge.

EIGHTH HOUSE/ELEVENTH HOUSE COUPLE

Your Karmic Path: Dramatic life/death events somehow play into the manifestation of your dreams and ambitions as a couple. There can be a profound awareness of your past-life ties, which can hold you back or propel you forward as a couple.

Strength: Friends and acquaintances are supportive of your relationship and understand your mutual goals and dreams.

Challenge: Friends and acquaintances may interfere in your relationship.

NINTH HOUSE/TWELFTH HOUSE COUPLE

Your Karmic Path: The student/teacher aspect of your relationship revolves around your worldview and the power that one of you has disowned. The karmic ties between you should be brought to the surface and, if possible, resolved so that you can move forward.

Strength: Through education, travel, and your spiritual bond, you're able to create something lasting.

Challenge: One of you may feel that some things should remain hidden or buried.

TENTH HOUSE/FIRST HOUSE COUPLE

Your Karmic Path: Issues about independence and career are at the crux of your path together. Resolve them, incorporate them into who you are as a couple—or be undone by them.

Strength: You both have the inner strength and inner resources to create a successful relationship.

Challenge: "Me first" may be a mantra for one of you.

ELEVENTH HOUSE/SECOND HOUSE COUPLE

Your Karmic Path: Integrating your values into your ideals in a genuine way is at the heart of your relationship. The student/teacher part of this equation revolves around issues concerning friends, groups, personal values, and money. It's not a particularly easy combination.

Strength: You have the capacity to become each other's support system.

Challenge: Disagreement about what's important in life could interfere with your relationship.

TWELFTH HOUSE/THIRD HOUSE COUPLE

Your Karmic Path: Most combinations with the eighth and twelfth houses seem to have an awareness of past-life ties. This combination does, too, and it's likely to revolve around personal power—and its absence—and how that is communicated to your partner. Your path together lies in communication.

Strength: Metaphysical awareness is your greatest strength—use it!

Challenge: Interference by siblings, relatives, and neighbors could be a problem.

CREATIVE PARTNERSHIP

FOUR SIGNS APART

A creative partnership is one in which both individuals are free to use their respective abilities and creative strengths to achieve their potential. Granted, this should be one of the goals of any partnership. But astrologically speaking, this kind of partnership is more likely between people whose Sun signs are trine to each other—or share the same element.

If you're an Aries, for instance, then both Sagittarius and Leo are trine to your sign, or separated by 120 degrees. A trine, like a sextile, indicates an easy exchange of energy, a flow. Check Table 6 on the following page.

TABLE 6: TRINES

Your Sun Sign	Trine to
♈ Aries	Leo, Sagittarius
♉ Taurus	Virgo, Capricorn
♊ Gemini	Aquarius, Libra
♋ Cancer	Scorpio, Pisces
♌ Leo	Sagittarius, Aries
♍ Virgo	Taurus, Capricorn
♎ Libra	Gemini, Aquarius
♏ Scorpio	Cancer, Pisces
♐ Sagittarius	Aries, Leo
♑ Capricorn	Virgo, Taurus
♒ Aquarius	Gemini, Libra
♓ Pisces	Cancer, Scorpio

One caveat about the ease of trine relationships: There are always exceptions. Although I've known plenty of trine couples who symbolize the epitome of creative partnerships, I've also met some who would be better off divorced. Sometimes, the trine creates so much ease that the partners inadvertently stir up problems and challenges, almost as if they need trials and tribulations to keep the relationship exciting.

Generally, though, two signs that share the same element are compatible because their overall energy is the same. They begin at the same place. Fire signs are dynamic, active people; earth signs are practical and grounded; air signs are intellectual and communicative; and water signs are emotional and intuitive.

John Lennon, a Libra, and Yoko Ono, an Aquarius, are a good example of an air trine relationship. Even though they had their share of challenges—fame, substance abuse, infidelities—their partnership was primarily a creative one that centered around communication through music, writing, and performance. In the years since Lennon's assassination, Ono has continued to speak out against war with the message for which Lennon is remembered: "Give peace a chance."

Interestingly, another Beatle was involved in a trine relationship that seemed somewhat more stable than that of Lennon and Ono. Gemini Paul McCartney and Libra Linda Eastman spent twenty-nine years together and were allegedly inseparable. The only time they were apart was when McCartney spent ten days in a Tokyo jail for carrying marijuana. Linda was a photographer when they met and became a keyboarder and backup singer in two of McCartney's post-Beatle bands.

Sun Sign Combinations

*This section describes how you and your
partner relate to each other.*

♈♌

ARIES/LEO COUPLE

There's plenty of passion in this combination, and the passion can go a very long way toward mitigating the fiery emotional outbursts that are surely part of it. As fire signs, both Aries and Leo have quick tempers—but neither of them is known for holding a grudge. When they've blown, that's it. They move on.

Aries tends to be more independent than Leo (or thinks he is, at any rate) and often will be the leader in terms of creative ideas. It isn't that Aries is more inherently creative than Leo is, just that Aries, as a cardinal sign, needs to direct the show (or thinks that he does). In the same way that Aries needs to direct, Leo must shine in whatever she does. She must have the center stage in terms of the public. As long as Aries and Leo keep these two rules in mind, their creative partnership won't experience many bumps.

Their sexual relationship is filled with all the spit and fire you would expect from…well, two fire signs. Both are passionate people who also enjoy a lot of physical contact and expression—touching, hugging, holding hands. Any creative activities or projects in which they're both involved will only enhance their sexual relationship and their sexual appreciation of each other.

Aries tends to be more impulsive than Leo. "Let's go hiking today," Aries might suggest, expecting to leave in the next sixty seconds. But Leo has a few things to do before she leaves the house. She wants to make some calls, wash her gorgeous hair, or add a touch of makeup. After all, Leo is now going out into public and will be seen. If Leo is the male in the relationship, then the emphasis may be on clothes, his car, or his backpack—the things that reflect who he is. Leo is just as dynamic and excited about life as Aries is, but always in the back of her mind is that little voice that whispers, "Look your best."

Of the two, Leo usually has more patience than Aries does. The ram is always eager to push ahead into new experiences and terrain, and if he gets bored, he doesn't bother finishing what he starts. This may drive Leo nuts, as she hurries along behind Aries, soothing whomever the ram has angered on his way out the door. But when it's just the two of them, working feverishly on some creative project they've hatched, this combination is about as fine as they come for an equal and creative partnership.

♉ ♍

TAURUS/VIRGO COUPLE

In a creative partnership, these two earth signs usually finish what they start. Even when they're attracted to esoteric ideas, they bring the material to a practical, grounded level so that it's comprehensible to others, and they work at it until they get it right.

Virgo is the detail person in this partnership, and Taurus is the money person. If they stick to these roles, then it increases their chances of great success in a creative project. Taurus, ruled by Venus, has a deep interest in the arts and may have artistic talent himself. Virgo, ruled by Mercury, is a consummate communicator. If they can combine these talents in some way, the results may be extraordinary.

As earth signs, both Taurus and Virgo are health conscious—not necessarily health freaks, but instinctively aware of what nutritional and exercise programs are good for them. Taurus is more likely than Virgo to act on that awareness, however, particularly when it comes to exercise. Maybe it's Venus's rulership that pushes the bull to the gym or to yoga class, with the need to remain attractive. Virgo tends to live more in her head. But because she's a mutable sign—flexible—she'll be willing to go to the gym or to yoga because he does. She'll be willing to try. In return, she'll expect the bull to hit the bookstores with her, where she can while away hours, poking through displays and paging through books that interest her.

Neither sign is known for stretching the truth, so their communication with each other should remain open and honest. Virgo can be a bit more honest at times than Taurus likes, and sometimes her honesty is tinged with criticism. Taurus will listen and turn quiet and sullen for a while, absorbing what Virgo has said, then will put it behind him. But the next time Virgo begins to pick and criticize, Taurus will simply tune her out.

There are many ways to be creative in a partnership, and this one works best if they are both passionate about the project. For Virgo, this means engaging her mind; for Taurus, it means engaging his artistic sensibilities. A joint creative project won't be as satisfying if one of the partners is simply helping out. That's not the point of this partnership. Things have to be equal.

Sexually, this relationship doesn't have the fiery passions of a couple who are both fire signs. But it has something else—a quiet, profound, and often mystical connection, where sex becomes a conduit to something greater than either person. During sex, these two may sense their past-life connections and may even have flashes of insight about the specifics of those past lives.

Despite their common earth bond, Taurus and Virgo come to conclusions in different ways. When Taurus is confronted with a choice, the bull feels his way through it—not with his emotions, but with his body. Does he feel resistance in his body? Acquiescence? And then he goes with that feeling. A Virgo is more apt to allow the choices to move through her meticulously detailed mind and base her decision on logic rather than emotion. This could cause a few upsets in the relationship until both partners understand this process in each other.

Overall, this combination works well most of the time. Once you decide on your creative venue, you'll stick with it to the end.

♊ ♒

GEMINI/AQUARIUS COUPLE

The mental attraction between these two is intriguing to observe. Both have erratic intellects that run parallel for a few miles, then intersect, then separate and run parallel, then intersect again. It's like a crazy dance that would drive a couple of earth signs crazy. But these two thrive on the intellectual excitement they bring to each other. And they always have something to talk about—the state of the Union, books, movies, baseball, the cosmos. No topic is forbidden, and nothing is too small or too large to bring to the dinner table.

If there is a dinner table. Gemini would just as soon eat on the run, but Aquarius, despite his erratic mindset and often quirky ideas, likes certain traditions he can count on.

In the creative sense, this combination is all about ideas and communication, and in one way or another, any joint project will be geared toward communication. If, for instance, the joint project is raising a family, then be assured that with a Gemini and an Aquarius as parents, the kids will be encouraged to express who they are.

The duality inherent in Gemini won't bother Aquarius. For him, the twins keep things exciting and interesting. He may even come to consider them as separate, distinct personalities, which they sometimes are. In turn, Gemini loves Aquarius's quirky, visionary mind, his oddball ideas, and his deep humanity. These individual quirks of theirs don't end as soon as they enter the bedroom. Aquarius and Gemini talk when the spirit moves them, which is often, and that intimacy bleeds over into their sex lives.

Gemini can talk circles around most signs, but Aquarius is quick to decipher the real meaning of whatever the twins are saying. In the same way, Aquarius may wander off into one of his discourses about this or that, and Gemini is quick to direct him to the point. These two usually understand each other's methods.

It's difficult to say which of them recognizes past-life connections first. Aquarius's mind doesn't recognize boundaries of time and space, and he's just as likely to come up with a past life they shared as well as a future life they will share. Gemini may catch glimpses now and then or may have long, intricate dreams in which past-life ties are laid out as intricately as a mosaic. For the most part, Gemini is more interested in the here and now.

♋︎♏︎

CANCER/SCORPIO COUPLE

This combination is creatively charged because both signs have strong intuition, terrific imaginations, and intense emotions. They are highly protective of themselves, their loved ones, their families, and their home. Even the creatures that symbolize these signs—the crab and the scorpion—have strong, protective exoskeletons.

There's no way to predict what these two may produce in a creative sense. Cancer would prefer to do whatever it is from home, and Scorpio just wants to be independent enough so that he doesn't have to answer to an outside boss. If their creativity revolves around home and children, a distinct possibility, then their kids are sure to be exceptionally intuitive and perhaps overly protective as well. In the best of all possible scenarios, their kids will have a solid understanding of the link between emotions and health.

Of the two, Scorpio is the more intense; to him, life is serious business. Life may be serious to Cancer, too, but she has a lighter sense of things, a way to place things in perspective. She's capable of teasing Scorpio into a lighter mood. However, if she does it by making fun of him, Scorpio won't forget it and will get even.

Both signs have startling memories—perhaps not for dates and historical events, but for emotional details and the texture of personal experiences. If you ask Cancer about her childhood, chances are she can recite chapter and verse what she did on her fifth birthday, as long as there was a strong emotional component to it. You might ask Scorpio the same thing and even though he remembers, he'll clam up completely. Of the two, Scorpio is by far the more secretive. You have to win his loyalty before he'll trust you. The crab, a fellow water sign, knows precisely how to win that trust by going with the flow.

In the bedroom, there are fireworks, but not as there are for fire signs. It's unlikely that these two chat at all in the bedroom, as air signs might.

If anything, the bedroom chat between these two water signs occurs at a telepathic level, where a touch communicates tomes. Sex is also a conduit into their past-life connections. Both bring an awareness of the soul's sum total when they come into this life, and that may be part of what they bring to their creativity.

♌♐ LEO/SAGITTARIUS COUPLE

This combination, like that of the Aries/Leo couple, is fiery and passionate, but with some distinct differences.

In the Aries/Leo combination, Aries usually emerges as the leader; in this combination, the division isn't as clear. Sagittarius loves to think she's the leader, but more than often not, Leo is. Leo is equally deluded; after all, he's king of the jungle! In other words, with these two, no one wins an argument. Good thing, too, because this sort of combined energy should be creative, not argumentative.

Creative of what? That depends on the mutual interests these two bring to their relationship. Leo enjoys virtually anything that puts her on center stage, where she can shine, get involved, or throw herself into a project. Sagittarius is forever on the lookout for the larger picture, purpose, motive, or truth.

Maybe Leo is an actress and Sagittarius is the location scout. Maybe Sagittarius is the writer and Leo is the publisher. The give and take between these two must be based on individual strengths, not on whose will is strongest. If these two play politics in their relationship, then it will be one of those trines that fail.

One possible glitch in this relationship has to do with Sagittarius's bluntness and Leo's need for approval. A steady diet of Sadge's bluntness ("The first time I saw you, you were fifteen pounds lighter.") or a constant need for approval from Leo ("How'd I do? Do I look okay? Huh? Huh?") won't do for these two. If either partner is ever made to feel like an appendage, rather than an equal, then these two should simply end it and go their separate ways. But if they can work their way around these differences, then together they can create something magnificent and lasting.

♍ ♑

VIRGO/CAPRICORN COUPLE

These two earth signs are as snug as peas in a pod. Both shoulder responsibility with admirable staunchness and are steady, reliable workers. You generally don't find either one calling in sick to work just because it's dark and cold outside when the alarm clock goes off.

A creative partnership between these two can go anywhere. They will pursue their creative projects with a stolid determination that only Taurus can equal, and by the time they're ready to launch their product or idea or whatever it is, they'll have a plan and a strategy. They are loyal to their ideals and passions, and they are usually loyal to each other, too.

They share not only a sense of reliability but also a certain propriety about the ways in which they conduct themselves. They are generally refined individuals who loathe crudeness and try to follow the rules of whatever society they live in. Virgos have been accused of being prissy, obsessively tidy people and Capricorns have been accused of being nakedly ambitious. Both take umbrage at such descriptions, which are rarely true, and sympathize with each other when they're wrongly accused. Yes, some Virgos are neat freaks and some Capricorns are ambitious, but these are gross generalities.

Their outward appearances are often deceptive. Virgo, who at times appears to be cool and aloof, and Capricorn, who can seem detached, have a harmonious sex life. Both can be as passionate as fire signs. They don't need sex as a conduit into past-life memories, though. They're both aware of the karmic connections early on in the relationship. And neither is likely to run from it. "Karma?" they ask in unison. "That's just one more responsibility. Sure, we're up to the task!"

The beauty of the attraction between these two is that once they fall for each other, they probably will legalize it and resolve their karma within the parameters of a deeply committed relationship.

♎ ♊

LIBRA/GEMINI COUPLE

If you're an outsider eavesdropping on these two air signs, a typical conversation might go something like this:

Gemini: "Do you want to go to the party tonight?"

Libra: "Sure. Do you?"

Gemini: "I guess. If you do."

Libra: "Maybe just the two of us should catch that new art film."

Gemini: "There's a bookstore near that theater. Let's go there."

Libra: "Great."

Gemini: "The party's going to be fun, though. Lots of different types of people."

Libra: "Okay, let's do the party. I'm game either way."

And so it goes, around and around, with Libra thinking that what she really wants to do is go to the party, but she knows that Gemini just wants to go a bookstore. The end result? They probably stay home, or Libra wins. Or maybe Gemini wins. Who knows? Libra wants to please, and Gemini hates to be pinned down, but each understands the other's mental gymnastics.

It's true that Libra can charm his way out of anything and that Gemini can talk her way out of a sticky situation. So when these two come together, the conversation is practically nonstop and, as with Aquarius and Gemini, no topic is forbidden. They talk till they drop, and when they aren't talking, they're thinking about talking or they simply are thinking. When these two collaborate on something creative, communication certainly will be involved in one way or another.

Neither sign is quick to anger, although both have flash points. If Gemini is criticized too often, picked at over what she considers to be silly, inconsequential things, she'll blow. But she, like Aries, rarely holds a grudge. Life is too short. Libra's flash point comes when he weighs and tries to balance events once too often. He is his own worst enemy in this regard.

Sex between these two air signs begins in the mind, with an idea or a concept on which the two agree. This ignites a kind of recognition of a kindred soul, a past-life relationship that has come around again. Both signs eagerly embrace that knowledge.

♍♓
SCORPIO/PISCES COUPLE

These two really inhabit two worlds—the world the rest of us live in and their own private little world, where others visit by invitation only. And this is true regardless of the context of the relationship and whether they are lovers, friends, siblings, parents, or children.

Scorpio, a fixed water sign, and Pisces, a mutable water sign, are telepathically connected, the same way that any water trine is. The nature of water is to assume the shape of the vessel into which it's poured, and when Pisces is poured into Scorpio, or vice versa, their knowledge of each other is complete. This isn't to say that they are the same person or that complete fusion is what they're after, but let's face it, fusion is a terrific aid to mutual understanding.

So what form might creativity take in such a partnership? It's impossible to predict. But given the Scorpio inclination to get to the absolute bottom line about anything and the vast imagination of Pisces, here are some educated guesses: a research company, a private investigation firm, a cosmetics or perfume line, a clothing line, music, writing, the arts, or acting. The sky really is the limit with this combination.

However, there are caveats, as usual. Thanks to Scorpio's emotional intensity and Pisces's deep compassion, things may not go as smoothly as they could. Pisces may end up bending far too much to accommodate Scorpio's demands—"You have to earn my trust, this is my money, my house, my whatever"—and so the two end up like Scorpio Richard Burton and Pisces Liz Taylor, who married each other twice and still couldn't get it right. Sometimes with this combination, there's so much closeness that it's impossible to live a normal life outside of it.

The primary difference between these two, and it's a big difference, is that many Scorpios seem to be born knowing who they are and many Pisceans are in a constant state of becoming…well, someone.

But when Scorpio bolsters Pisces's self-confidence and Pisces fills Scorpio with faith, when each provides what the other lacks, then this combination works beautifully.

↗ ♈

SAGITTARIUS/ARIES COUPLE

This is the third of the fire combinations, and in some ways, it may be the most problematic for a trine partnership. Here we have restless, impatient, independent Aries trying to boss around nomadic, independent Sadge. Or we have an expansive, boisterous Sadge trying to cram his or her religious beliefs down Aries's throat.

If these two can get past all that (and they can), then the combination works like the proverbial charm. As a team, they have such an abundance of sheer physical energy that when they enter a room filled with strangers, conversations pause. Eyes turn their way. Sadge and Aries eat up the attention, then grow bored with it and may wander away from the crowd to continue the conversation they began yesterday or five minutes ago. And what a conversation it is. Sadge has plans to travel the world and that's fine with Aries, as long as he can tag along, too. Never mind that they may go their separate ways once they're on the road; both are independent enough to do that and as long as they trust each other, there's no cause for jealousy. Besides, they'll meet up somewhere along the way, and their lovemaking will be explosively passionate.

Even if they're staying in their own backyard, these two find adventure and excitement in their relationship. Good thing, too, because boredom is anathema to both Aries and Sadge. When they pour their considerable joint energies into a creative project, business, or lifestyle, they don't have to answer to anyone but each other. This makes them happier, and happy campers are essential in this relationship.

Leadership issues may surface from time to time. But because both signs are outspoken, there's no lasting harm done here. In fact, once these two get past egotism and selfishness, they're a force to be reckoned with.

♑ ♉

CAPRICORN/TAURUS COUPLE

This double earth combination works well most of the time. Even though cardinal sign Capricorn may try to boss Taurus around, the bull knows when to dig in his heels and refuse to budge. And in the event that Taurus gets bossy, the goat simply walks off to engage herself in something else until Taurus has seen the light.

These two are simpaticos, comrades, and coconspirators whose visions of life are so similar that when they fall for each other, they can map out a common strategy for what they want to achieve as a team. In their creative endeavors, there is no predicting where their combined energies might take them, except straight to the top of whatever they do.

If there are problems in this partnership, they don't stem around the usual issues that trip up many couples. Money, for instance, shouldn't be an issue. These practical earth signs known how to save, but they also how to enjoy what they earn. The issue of children shouldn't be a problem, either. Remember: Earth signs tend to be loving parents. If there are any challenges, they're likely to show up in Capricorn's occasional emotional coldness and Taurus's occasional selfishness.

With these two, there's likely to be a metaphysical bond that neither of them can explain away. It may surface during lovemaking, when they feel their past-life ties strongly. Even if they never consciously explore these ties, their karmic connection keeps them centered and together.

♒ ♎

AQUARIUS/LIBRA COUPLE

This is the third air sign combination. Because it's also a fixed/cardinal sign combination, the issues that surface between Aquarius and Libra often center around leadership. Libra figures she's in charge, but when she tries to throw her weight around with Aquarius, the water bearer won't put up with it and simply removes himself from the situation. Or if Aquarius is confrontational about something and the argument gets ugly (unlikely, but it's been known to happen), then Libra is blasted by the terrible disharmony of it all and has to skulk away to lick her wounds for a while. Other than that, these two shouldn't encounter any major relationship issues. They have a mental camaraderie that keeps them in synch with each other and allows them to get over disagreements quickly.

With Aquarius's quirky and often brilliant ideas and approach to life and Libra's knack for networking and charming her way through anything, these two can go in any creative direction that suits them. The arts, computers, electronics, metaphysics, public relations…the exploration is what matters. When their passions and curiosity are fully engaged, when they're a truly equal team, the journey sweeps them up and takes them to places they never imagined.

Sexually, these two are well suited. Libra enjoys being enjoyed by her partner, and Aquarius has all the right vocabulary to seduce and romance her. However, Aquarius sometimes lives so deeply in his head that the rush of ideas follows him into the bedroom. And occasionally, Libra gets held up answering phone calls and e-mail messages from her vast network of acquaintances; by the time she reaches the bedroom, Aquarius has fallen asleep.

Libra may waffle on decisions more than Aquarius likes. But Aquarius, as a fixed sign, may be more stubborn than Libra likes. In the end, it all balances out and these two idiosyncratic individuals somehow make it all work.

♓♋

PISCES/CANCER COUPLE

These signs are probably most content when it's just the two of them, swimming through the private little world they create. Both are moody, changeable, and deeply intuitive, if not downright psychic. They don't have to say much in each other's company to communicate. A touch, a smile, a quick laugh is enough to establish their psychic connection. Sometimes, they don't even need that.

Cancer, ruled by the Moon, and Pisces, ruled by Neptune, the god of the oceans, are equally secretive, sensitive, and changeable. Both have excellent imaginations and an innate sense of their connection to an inner vastness. Neither one is a risk taker; yet, when it comes to creative endeavors, they are willing to take emotional and psychic risks.

The major challenge with this combination is escapism and procrastination. The escapism part of this equation can involve alcohol, drugs, or even sex. With Pisces, there can be a tendency toward victimization if the fish is lacking in self-confidence. Both signs can be procrastinators, the typical *mañana, mañana* sort who just can't see the point of moving forward right this second.

Cancer can be more possessive than Pisces is, but Pisces has a tougher time making decisions. Cancer tends to be more money conscious also, which may drive Pisces nuts when she's in the mood for a shopping spree. Of the two, Cancer is the true homebody, and within his home he likes a predictable routine. His home, after all, isn't just his castle; it's also an extension of his soul. Pisces craves change, though, and the more of it, the better, but what else would you expect from a dual mutable sign? So when Cancer sinks into his home, Pisces should have a place that she goes or an activity (or several) that she does that satisfies her need for change.

Other than these challenges, which certainly don't even approach insurmountable, these two can enter realms that are closed to the rest of us—and bring back extraordinary tales!

Sun/North Node Connections

T he descriptions below address both variations of a combination. If you have a first house Sun and your partner's North Node falls in your fifth house, or if your Sun is in the fifth house and your partner's North Node falls in your first, then the first description applies to both.

The Sun/North Node combinations describe your karmic path as a couple, the strengths and challenges you face in the relationship and how you and your partner evolve through the relationship to achieve your individual potential. However, you can apply the descriptions to anyone in your life.

When astrologers compare a couple's chart, they often use a biwheel, with one partner's chart in the inner wheel and the other person's chart in the outer wheel. This enables you to see where your partner's planets fall in your houses and which of your planets are hit. The ways in which your partner's planets impact yours describes what your partner brings to the relationship. When your partner's chart is in the inner wheel and yours is in the biwheel, it indicates what you bring to your partner in the relationship. Always start with your natal Sun, which is the basic archetype of who you are.

By now, you've either downloaded your and your partner's charts from the Internet or have used one of the blank charts in the back of the book to place your Sun and North Node and those of your partner in the appropriate houses. So read on!

FIRST HOUSE/FIFTH HOUSE COUPLE

Your Karmic Path: As a couple, you've chosen a creative life in which you chart your own course and are your own boss. You become more aware of how your beliefs create your reality. You can be pioneers in whatever you do. Children may play into this creative equation.

Strength: You're certain of your joint abilities.

Challenge: You need to be more cooperative.

SECOND HOUSE/SIXTH HOUSE COUPLE

Your Karmic Path: As a couple, your path is to walk your talk, so that it's reflected in all aspects of your life, especially in your daily work and in the ways you tend to your health. In other words, if you're an avid animals rights activist, this should be reflected in your choice of foods, clothing, and so on. Talk must be backed up by action.

Strength: You're willing to work hard for what you want.

Challenge: Your challenge is to keep from becoming a workaholic.

THIRD HOUSE/SEVENTH HOUSE COUPLE

Your Karmic Path: Communication is an intimate part of your partnership as a couple as well as your business and professional partnerships. As a couple, you can make allies of your enemies. Siblings, relatives, and even the neighborhood in which you live somehow figure into your joint karmic path.

Strength: Your commitment to getting your message out is your greatest strength.

Challenge: You need to work on being nondogmatic in your communication.

FOURTH HOUSE/EIGHTH HOUSE COUPLE

Your Karmic Path: Family and shared resources figure into your path as a couple. The manifestation of these qualities depends on the scope and strength of your free will as individuals and as a couple. Metaphysics or esoteric thought may be one of the areas that you explore together.

Strength: Your generous spirit and spiritual awareness help you do the right thing at the right time.

Challenge: Avoid becoming bitter if things don't work out as you hoped.

FIFTH HOUSE/NINTH HOUSE COUPLE

Your Karmic Path: Your spiritual or philosophical beliefs are an intricate part of your creative endeavors. Higher education and international travel figure into the larger picture of your karmic path.

Strength: Your awareness of spiritual and metaphysical truths is a tremendous aid in achieving your potential as a couple.

Challenge: Your pursuit of pleasure will distract you from your path.

SIXTH HOUSE/TENTH HOUSE COUPLE

Your Karmic Path: As a couple, you achieve your career ambitions through a meticulous attention to your daily work, or vice versa. With this particular configuration, there may be a lot of work with the public through charities, volunteer work, or your career.

Strength: Your commitment is your greatest strength.

Challenge: You need to keep your ambition from overpowering your karmic path.

SEVENTH HOUSE/ELEVENTH HOUSE COUPLE

Your Karmic Path: Through your partnership, you work to make the world a better place. You network with others who share your ideals and understand that every mass movement begins with the individual.

Strength: Your belief in metaphysical principles is your greatest strength.

Challenge: Friends may become a hindrance rather than a help.

EIGHTH HOUSE/TWELFTH HOUSE COUPLE

Your Karmic Path: As a couple, you explore metaphysical principles and beliefs to deepen your own psychic and intuitive abilities. You share your resources with others and work behind the scenes to effect change in the larger world.

Strength: Your strength is in your combined intuition.

Challenge: Isolation may become a problem.

NINTH HOUSE/FIRST HOUSE COUPLE

Your Karmic Path: Your exploration of ideas, spiritual belief systems, and foreign countries and cultures enhances your self-knowledge. As a couple, you use this knowledge to create your mutual reality.

Strength: Your curiosity and determination are great strengths.

Challenge: Distractions, and yes, there are plenty of them, may be a challenge. Sometimes, couples with this configuration are restless nomads who see every country there is to see and still don't understand what they've been looking for.

TENTH HOUSE/SECOND HOUSE COUPLE

Your Karmic Path: Either your personal values are reflected in your career choices or your career choices help shape your personal values. Whichever it is, this is both an individual and a team effort. As a couple, you must commit first to the relationship, and then to whatever comes next.

Strength: As a team, you have a clear sense of where you're headed.

Challenge: Make sure ambition and/or greed don't consume you.

ELEVENTH HOUSE/THIRD HOUSE COUPLE

Your Karmic Path: Your ideas and thoughts are powerful enough to reach the masses. As a couple, your path is to figure out how best to communicate, and then do it.

Strength: Your strength lies in your vast network of contacts and communication skills.

Challenge: Often, too much is going on at once. Set your priorities.

TWELFTH HOUSE/FOURTH HOUSE COUPLE

Your Karmic Path: By healing yourselves, you heal each other. You tend to be private people who work out your challenges in private. It's important not to be recluses, however. Even the happiest people occasionally need contact with others.

Strength: You enjoy working behind the scenes.

Challenge: Strive not to get lost in your own issues. What you learn should be shared with others.

MAGICIAN

FIVE SIGNS APART

This category sounds esoteric and intriguing, but it can be tricky. Like the square and the opposition (chapters 8 and 11), it should be navigated with great care and awareness.

Signs and planets that are separated by 150 degrees—five signs apart, in other words—are quincunx to each other. At one time, this aspect was considered a minor one, but in recent years, some astrologers have come to treat it as a major aspect. It's a stressful aspect, but not in the same sense as a square, which causes friction, or an opposition, which creates confrontation. The quincunx requires an inner adjustment of some kind, a subtle psychological shift.

When I was casting around for a title for this chapter, I tried to find a word that expressed the qualities necessary to navigate this aspect successfully in a relationship. After all, Sun signs or planets that are quincunx to each other don't share the same element or quality, so they don't have much in common astrologically. I finally settled on "magician" because it implies that each partner must bring a nonlinear way of perceiving to the relationship, a kind of magical approach.

Check out Table 7 below for the signs that are quincunx to yours.

TABLE 7: QUINCUNXES

Your Sun Sign	Quincunx to
♈ Aries	Virgo, Scorpio
♉ Taurus	Libra, Sagittarius
♊ Gemini	Scorpio, Capricorn
♋ Cancer	Sagittarius, Aquarius
♌ Leo	Capricorn, Pisces
♍ Virgo	Aquarius, Aries
♎ Libra	Pisces, Taurus
♏ Scorpio	Aries, Gemini
♐ Sagittarius	Taurus, Cancer
♑ Capricorn	Gemini, Leo
♒ Aquarius	Cancer, Virgo
♓ Pisces	Leo, Libra

In quincunx relationships, there seems to be an almost visceral sexual attraction and, quite often, a spontaneous recognition that you have known this person in other lives. Recognition of this sort, of course, depends on how self-aware a person is, but generally signs that are quincunx to each other feel the connection.

Sun Sign Combinations

This section describes how you and your
partner relate to each other.

♈ ♍

ARIES/VIRGO COUPLE

The initial attraction between these two very different signs may be due precisely to those differences. Virgo is attracted to the ram's courage, impulsiveness, and instinctive love of life. Aries is attracted to Virgo's precision, her penchant for details, and her willingness to work without complaint and do what has to be done. The sexual chemistry grows out of their differences. Odd, yes, but this isn't an ordinary relationship.

Virgo brings out the kindness in Aries, the part of him that pulls over to the side of the road to give a homeless man money. And Aries brings out these same qualities in Virgo, the ability to listen to a friend in need and to offer advice, her couch, or whatever is needed.

All this aside, daily life can be trying for these two when they're involved with each other. Aries may accuse Virgo of being too critical; Virgo may accuse Aries of being too selfish. Both observations are true, and yet not true. That's where the magic comes in.

We frequently are attracted to people who convey some unexpressed facet of ourselves. So the next time Virgo criticizes Aries, he must detach emotionally from the criticism and try to determine whether what Virgo says is true. Has he been critical of others? And if so, for what? Is it possible that the very thing for which he criticizes others is something that he dislikes in himself? Granted, Aries isn't known for his introspection. But when his heart is involved, he'll do whatever he has to.

Virgo, on the other hand, is a master of self-analysis and self-criticism, so introspection isn't a problem for her. But still, she doesn't like it when Aries refers to her as prissy or uptight and frets that perhaps she has been prissy and uptight lately. She'll strive to correct these things in herself, particularly if she has decided that Aries is worth it.

In both cases, ego has to be set aside, and Aries and Virgo must enter the unknown armed with nothing but trust—a magician's initiation.

Sexually, these two should get along well. The passion of Aries excites Virgo, and her quiet directness is a turn-on for him. It's fine with Virgo if Aries wants to run off on some adventure with her now and then. She needs her solitude, and he needs his independence the way horses need hay. And it's these periods when they're apart that sweeten their reunion and keep the relationship magical.

♉ ♎

TAURUS/LIBRA COUPLE

Both signs are ruled by Venus, which at least gives them something in common. They share a love of art, music, literature, and beauty. They are both romantics, although in different ways.

That said, their differences may be dramatic. Libra has trouble making up his mind. It's all his fairness and balance issues that interfere. Should he go to work at seven or at eight? Should he wear a suit or go casual? And he doesn't hesitate expressing all these various possibilities to Taurus, who could care less. The typical bull, male or female, tends to be reticent and somewhat self-contained. He or she doesn't need to discuss every little possibility; the bull makes a decision, then sticks to it. No waffling.

Taurus resists engaging in any activity that seems to have no purpose. However, when the bull is convinced that something or someone is worthwhile, there is no sign more determined or more relentless in pursuing what he wants. Libra has trouble understanding the Taurean determination. Libra can be determined, yes, but not like this. In Libra's world, it's better to charm your way toward whatever you want.

So where does the magician enter into this picture? Listen up. Aries and Virgo must shift their perspectives slightly and enter into some new and unfamiliar world with little more than faith to back them. But with these two, the magic has to be ignited in communication. Taurus must be more flexible (not especially easy for a fixed sign); Libra must be more willing to listen to what she says, when she says it. If he learns to listen, he may learn something about her that has escaped him until now! And Libra must include Taurus in her plans. When she's about to hurry across a room to greet someone from her vast network of friends, she should take Taurus's hand and bring him along. When she's about to do something deceptive because she doesn't want to upset Taurus (or break his heart), she must check herself and then be honest. There's magic in honesty.

Another potential challenge in this relationship, where a little magic could work wonders, is that Libra, as a cardinal sign, figures she's in charge. If she's smart, she'll quickly learn that no one pushes the bull around. He may nod and agree with what she's saying, but when she tells him he absolutely must do something and he disagrees, he'll refuse. And that will be that. End of discussion; end of story. And if she does it enough times, end of relationship. Neither partner should ever assume the other will do something. They need to talk first, and discuss but not argue.

Of course, there probably aren't many outright arguments with these two. Neither likes disharmony. But if too much goes unsaid, if bitterness and resentment begin to fester, then the explosion that will eventually follow won't be pretty, and both Taurus and Libra will be wounded. These two need to be magical in their choice of words.

♊♏
GEMINI/SCORPIO COUPLE

Gemini meets his match with Scorpio. It's impossible to talk circles around a Scorpio because she always sees through it. It's her gift and her curse. So Gemini can forget playing words games with Scorpio. She either likes you or she doesn't. She's a fixed sign, remember, and deeply intuitive, and she isn't easily fooled by the mental and verbal dexterity of the twins.

However, Scorpio is intrigued by Gemini's duality. There's so much to discover and uncover, so many twists and turns in that weird mind, so much exhaustive movement. Just who is this person, really? And Scorpio will take as much time as she needs to find out.

Gemini may not understand Scorpio's long, moody silences or may not be able to decipher her penetrating stares. But he's smitten. The attraction is magnetic, and he's the bits of iron, pulled into that aura of mystery and silence. But once he's in the aura, he is haunted by Scorpio's world—the strangeness, the language, and the deep resonance with otherworldly concerns. And the lovemaking—who could deny the beauty and intensity of it? But over time, Gemini discovers he's flummoxed by Scorpio, that even his mercurial mind can't travel every twisting corridor, every maze in the Scorpio soul. But maybe that's how it should be for these two, each of them perpetually puzzled and intrigued by the other.

Their differences are vast, their approaches to life at opposite extremes. But the magic is there right from the start. However, once they've been together for a while, he will find her need for control downright irritating, maybe even infuriating. And she will find his need for diversity utterly maddening. But if we stick to the theory that we often attract what we ourselves have not expressed, then perhaps Scorpio needs to lighten up and Gemini needs to be more focused. Or something. Only they will be able to figure out who needs what and why.

In many ways, this mutable air sign and fixed water sign embody the magician's journey from the world of the ordinary to the world of magic.

♋ ♐
CANCER/SAGITTARIUS COUPLE

Water and fire. In what neutral territory can they possibly meet? Where can they thrive and flourish? Cancer is a homebody; Sagittarius is a nomad. Cancer treasures ties to family, and Sadge, though he loves his family, loves his cosmic search even more. Cancer is moody; Sadge is generally the steady optimist. These differences just go on and on.

Yet, when these two are attracted to each other, they feel their past-life ties at some deep and primal level. Their souls seize up in recognition.

Their hearts shift gears, their minds shiver, they *know*.

In some weird way, Cancer and Sadge manage to fill in each other's blanks. Sadge suddenly finds magic and adventure in his home life; Cancer suddenly finds life outside her personal space. Sadge dives into the Cancerian waters in search of truth, and Cancer dives into Sadge's relentless search for truth with a tenacity that only the crab has in great abundance.

Cancer is often possessive, which drives Sadge crazy and pushes him away. But Sadge secretly loves the way Cancer dotes on him, and even if she won't share her deepest secrets with him, well, he's got plenty of time to dig them out.

Sadge's sense of adventure and his spontaneity are beacons that Cancer holds in high esteem. Cancer's ability to keep a secret is something that Sadge admires. He loves talking with her, picking her brain, and all the while he's trying to understand how she knows things she has no business knowing. He respects her intuitive certainty, and she respects his search for the larger picture, the bigger truths. But in daily life it gets complicated very quickly. His bluntness hurts her. Her possessiveness and pouting and mood changes make his nuts. His lack of responsibility, her excessively close ties to her family, his independence, her possessiveness…and on and on it goes, the ego shouting, the spirit withering.

The magic in this relationship must enter in a subtle way, with each partner willing to reach fully into the other's world, if only for a while.

♌♑
LEO/CAPRICORN COUPLE

I know several people who have this configuration in their birth charts—a Capricorn Sun and a Leo Moon, for instance. Or a Leo Sun with a Capricorn Ascendant. It's a tough combination. But in a birth chart, you're dealing with your own energies and conflicts, and one way or another, you must resolve the differences within your own life. But when another person enters the picture, things get confusing very quickly.

A fixed fire sign and a cardinal earth sign have practically nothing in common. Leo is ruled by the glorious Sun, and Capricorn is ruled by stern and regimented Saturn. Although it's true that fire can consume the things of the earth, a handful of dirt on a campfire smothers it fast. You get the idea here. This combination isn't easy or simple.

Leo lives for today, and Capricorn lives for the day that he reaches the top of the mountain, whatever that mountain may be. Leo must shine; Capricorn must achieve. Leo must be worshiped, coddled, and stroked, but Capricorn must be hugged and appreciated. Okay, so where can these two meet each other halfway?

Within. As strange as it sounds, these two can create an inner, private world where the trappings of society and the larger world just don't matter. Well, that's not quite true. The outer world always matters—after all, thinks Leo, that's where the audience is, and yes, Capricorn agrees, that's where the power lies. But if they can create a private place when they are together, if they can create a certain magical place—like Hogwarts, perhaps?—where the rules are subject to the whims and surprises of magic itself, then this combination works. The challenge, though, is creating this special place.

The creation of this place becomes their joint project. They make up the rules, the roles, and the magic. They become the creators. And they take the journey willingly.

♍ ♒
VIRGO/AQUARIUS COUPLE

The one quality these two have in common is the ability to communicate. Even though Virgo is an earth sign, she's ruled by Mercury, the planet that symbolizes communication. And Aquarius, as an air sign, is all about communication. It's a solid basis for a relationship, and yet, they probably disagree on just about everything else.

Generally, Virgo has a tidy, organized mind and Aquarius has a quirky mind. Virgo remembers details and Aquarius is lucky if he remembers where he put his car keys. Virgo frets; Aquarius shrugs. There are always exceptions, particularly if Virgo has a Moon or Ascendant in Aquarius or if Aquarius has a Moon or Ascendant in Virgo. But we're talking only about Sun signs here and broad archetypal patterns.

Because Aquarius is ruled by Uranus, the planet of genius and sudden, unexpected change, he is extremely unpredictable in his behavior and interests, and in just about every other way, too. He won't have any problem, though, with interjecting some magic into his relationship with Virgo. No other sign is as well equipped to see the world from a completely different perspective than the rest of us. Virgo, as a mutable sign, is perfectly willing to play around with perceptual changes as well. So when Aquarius suggests doing something totally outrageous, Virgo embraces the opportunity (or should). When Virgo suggests a vacation to a Caribbean resort—instead of hiking the Incan trail—Aquarius should embrace the opportunity to do something he wouldn't think of doing on his own.

This quirkiness of Aquarius makes him sexually appealing to Virgo, and her quiet honesty does the same to him. Sex isn't their challenge. In fact, in bed, they get along just fine. It's through sex and love that they discover they have far more in common than they thought.

Aquarius's independence might be an issue with other signs, but it probably isn't with Virgo. She likes her time alone and enjoys her solitude, and if Aquarius feels like taking off on a humanitarian trip to some far-flung corner of the world, she's fine with that. In the same way, when Virgo heads out to a writer's convention by herself, Aquarius is okay with that, too.

In the end, Aquarius's visionary qualities and Virgo's mercurial mind blend well despite what most astrologers say. After all, we write our own scripts in life, right?

♎♓
LIBRA/PISCES COUPLE

One quality these two signs have in common is the inability to make a quick decision. For Libra, it's due to a need to balance everything and to please everyone. For Pisces, it's due to the perennial struggle between mind and heart. So when they come together in a romantic relationship, one of them needs to take charge, otherwise nothing will ever get done.

Libra, as the cardinal sign, is the one more likely to take charge, unless Pisces has a strong fire Moon or Ascendant. But regardless of who's in charge, Libra and Pisces are intrigued by each other. They may never understand each other completely, but so what? That's part of the attraction. Pisces, a mutable sign—the more flexible and adaptable of the two—must be careful not to bend over backward to accommodate herself to Libra's demands. Libra, whose life often reads like an advertising slogan—"We aim to please"—should strive not to be so eager to please that she loses herself in the process.

That said, these two shouldn't have any problem communicating, even if they're coming from vastly different places. Pisces enjoys Libra's ability to argue the many sides of a given issue, and Libra appreciates the fish's ability to see the mystical and the sacred within the mundane. They have no shortage of topics to discuss, of philosophies to share, of metaphysical ideas to brainstorm.

Pisces's ruler, Neptune, is said to be the higher octave of Venus, Libra's ruler, so it shouldn't come as any surprise that both signs are romantics. In fact, it's through romance that the magic in this relationship evolves. When Libra is driven to distraction by the constant vacillation of the fish and when Pisces is driven nuts by Libra's constant need for fairness and balance, they only have to think of the romance.

♏︎♈︎

SCORPIO/ARIES COUPLE

Scorpio is probably one of the few signs that can stand up to an Aries—not through shouting or physical strength, but simply by pinning Aries with a cold, silent, piercing glare. Even Aries learns rather quickly that Scorpio can't be cajoled, coaxed, or even threatened into doing something he doesn't want to do. And for an Aries in a relationship with a Scorpio, this can be a problem.

In romance, as in life, Aries acts impulsively, seizing what she wants. Scorpio, however, moves much more thoughtfully, carefully, and intuitively. Even when these two are in a relationship, Aries may wonder what's really going on inside Scorpio, what he really feels about her.

Scorpio won't have to wonder about the ram's affections, but everything else about her will puzzle him.

However, despite these glaring differences, Scorpio and Aries have one rather odd thing in common. Mars, which rules Aries, also co-rules Scorpio. The fiery warrior archetype that typifies Aries also typifies Scorpio, but the expression of that archetype is intuitive and emotional with Scorpio, rather than aggressive and dynamic, as it is with Aries. This helps create magic between them, as well as a sexual attraction that is magnetic and powerful. In fact, their myriad irritations with each other and their bafflement about each other vanish altogether when they're in bed.

The rest of the time, they must give each other a lot of latitude. It helps if each one is a good listener, and also listens to what the other *doesn't* say. Sometimes, especially with Scorpio, what's left unspoken is every bit as important as what is said.

This is one pair where the cardinal sign, Aries, probably thinks he's in charge, but it's intense, passionate Scorpio who is really calling the shots.

SAGITTARIUS/TAURUS COUPLE

These two move at such a different pace that it's astonishing they come together at all. Instead of the hare and the tortoise, though, we've got the centaur and the bull! The centaur gallops ahead, filled with his ideals and his desire for adventure, and the bull languishes in a field of sunlight and flowers, rather like Ferdinand in the children's story.

Sagittarius often is blunt to the point of hurting another, while Taurus, though honest, will shut up rather than create an unpleasant scene. This stony silence will infuriate Sadge, who wants to talk everything out. But the bull is a fixed sign and once he makes up his mind, that's it. He won't budge. If he's stubborn too long, Sadge simply removes herself from the equation and heads out on some adventure. Then Taurus may pine away, regretting his lapse of silence, but Sadge won't return until she's good and ready.

When the genders are reversed—Sadge is male and Taurus is female—the specifics don't change much. Sadge is still blunt and Taurus is still stubborn. These are archetypes we're talking about, patterns of energy and behavior, and they remain pretty much the same regardless of gender.

The magic in this combination is due to the rulers of the signs. Jupiter, Sadge's ruler, and Venus, which rules Taurus, are considered the most beneficent planets in the zodiac. Jupiter's expansiveness, optimism, and luck are also Sadge's; Venus's enjoyment of the arts, romance, and sensuality are also Taurus's. So even when things between the centaur and the bull seem doomed to failure, they are saved at the last moment by their ruling planets.

Sexually, most quincunx relationships seem to be magnetic and visceral. And this one certainly makes the grade. If they're smart, Sadge and Taurus will use their intimate time together to build a bridge to something greater.

♑ ♊
CAPRICORN/GEMINI COUPLE

Let's cut to the chase with this one. Dutiful, responsible Capricorn will never understand mercurial Gemini. It's difficult enough to understand one person, but when you're dealing regularly with two people, where do you begin? First, there's the exhaustion from trying to keep up with two of them—mental exhaustion because their minds dart around like gnats, and physical exhaustion because they move at the speed of light. Then there's pinning them down long enough to find out what they feel. How's that supposed to be done?

The view from where Gemini stands isn't much better. The goat won't budge, he has tunnel vision, he can be so cold, and what the heck is she doing in this relationship, anyway? Gemini thinks.

Given where they start from, it's astonishing they are attracted to each other at all. But it happens, and when it does, the repercussions on either side are fascinating. Gemini's intellect and interests trigger something in Capricorn; the goat's reserved, quiet way of moving through life offers Gemini a respite. Gemini, rarely an organized person, secretly admires Capricorn's organizational ability and may attempt to emulate it in her own life. Capricorn, who sometimes feels a need to bust out of his straight and narrow focus, secretly admires Gemini's ability to soar in the wind.

Capricorn finds Gemini exciting, and Gemini finds Capricorn stable and oddly soothing. At times, the twins will try Capricorn's patience, but there are plenty of times when the goat's stodginess grates on Gemini's nerves, too. That's when the magic is called for. Capricorn must put aside all notions about what he wants or doesn't want and listen to Gemini with an open mind and heart. Gemini must go utterly still and stay that way long enough to give Capricorn honest answers. Then the twins discover how soft and faithful the Capricorn heart can be, and Capricorn discovers a loyal, loving mate in the twins.

♒ ♋

AQUARIUS/CANCER COUPLE

These two are probably better off in an affair, where the heightened emotions of their encounters are kept at a fever pitch. If they try, instead, for a daily diet of each other, then Aquarius may find Cancer too clingy and possessive and Cancer may decide that Aquarius is just too...well, stubborn and weird.

However, in more evolved, spiritually aware types, both Cancer and Aquarius recognize a deeper resonance between them. Whether they call it a past-life connection or something else, they realize they have an appointment with each other this time around and it's best to explore it. Cancer's intuitive abilities fascinate Aquarius, as does anything having to do with the mind, and an exploration of metaphysics may be one of the deeper connections between them. In much the same way, Cancer is intrigued by the Aquarian ability to find cutting-edge trends, almost as though he can see into the future. And, quite often, he can. Humanitarian concerns, animal rights, and political activism are also areas of common interest for these two.

To get around their significant differences, Cancer should strive to be more open and communicative, and Aquarius should attempt to lay aside his opinions long enough to consider Cancer's suggestions and ideas. Even though their sex life may be erratic and unpredictable, it suits them both as long as they are sure they are okay with each other. And in evolved types, that okay is usually an unspoken acknowledgment that they are embracing a call to destiny.

♓☌♌

PISCES/LEO COUPLE

There's no question who's in charge with this combination. It's Leo the lion. He refuses to take a backseat to anyone. And that's really just fine with Pisces, as long as Leo doesn't throw his weight around in ways that are hurtful or insulting to her.

Never forget, however, that Pisces is a water sign, and water puts out fire. If Leo is wise, he will remember this when he gets on his high horse and tells her to do this or that. Pisces is perfectly willing to bend or become the vessel into which she is poured, though. In some instances, she bends too far and is mistreated (read: victim) and attempts to escape through activities related to her ruling planet, Neptune, namely alcohol or drug abuse. In a Pisces who's self-aware, though, escape isn't necessary. Her spiritual beliefs and her deep imagination provide a bulwark against the harsher realities of the world.

One place these two have common ground is that both tend toward insecurity. Leo's is expressed through a need for approval and Pisces's is expressed through an inability to make up her mind. But both behaviors stem from the same basic emotion: They feel they aren't good enough, smart enough, beautiful or talented enough. Once they realize this about each other, the relationship enters the realm of magic. They begin to believe in themselves because their partner believes in them.

Pisces is the most likely to recognize a past-life connection between them. She's able to see into that distant past when she puts her mind to it—through dreams, visions, meditation, art, or music. Leo may tune into the karmic connection through his creative work. He might, for instance, land a part in a play or movie where he plays a character who lived in a time when he knew Pisces.

These two would do well to be alert, always, for signs and synchronicities that mark their path through life together.

Sun/North Node
Connections

The descriptions below address both variations of a combination. If you have a first house Sun and your partner's North Node falls in your sixth house, or if your Sun is in the sixth house and your partner's North Node falls in your first house, then the first description applies to both.

The Sun/North Node combinations describe your karmic path as a couple—the strengths and challenges you face in the relationship and how you and your partner evolve through the partnership to achieve your individual potentials. However, you can apply the descriptions to anyone in your life.

When astrologers compare a couple's chart, they often use a biwheel, with one partner's chart in the inner wheel and the other person's chart in the outer wheel, just as you did in the practice at the beginning of part two. This enables you to see where your partner's planets fall in your houses and which of your planets are hit. The ways in which your partner's planets impact yours describes what your partner brings to the relationship. When your partner's chart is in the inner wheel and yours is in the biwheel, it indicates what you bring to your partner in the relationship. Always start with your natal Sun, which is the basic archetype of who you are.

By now, you've either downloaded your and your partner's charts from the Internet or have used one of the blank charts in the back of the book to place your Sun and North Node and those of your partner in the appropriate houses. So read on!

FIRST HOUSE/SIXTH HOUSE COUPLE

Your Karmic Path: As a couple, you must somehow incorporate your self-interests into your daily work, or vice versa. You need to walk the talk by living genuinely.

Strength: Your awareness of deeper realities bolsters your relationship.

Challenge: Self-interests taint your couple's path.

SECOND HOUSE/SEVENTH HOUSE COUPLE

Your Karmic Path: Your relationship must be in line with your personal values. If you and your partner are aware of your karmic connections, the previous statement will seem obvious. But if reincarnation is an area you haven't explored, then the relationship may need a significant adjustment in terms of worldviews and spiritual beliefs.

Strength: Your partnership is important to you, and it is something you're willing to work at.

Challenge: Money and finances may be an issue between you, or one of you is a workaholic.

THIRD HOUSE/EIGHTH HOUSE COUPLE

Your Karmic Path: Your relationship is about sharing your resources with others. This "sharing" could involve communication, books, knowledge, or even educational skills. Siblings, relatives, and neighbors play a large part in your karmic path as a couple.

Strength: You're willing participants in the deeper mysteries of life.

Challenge: You need to look at the big picture.

FOURTH HOUSE/NINTH HOUSE COUPLE

Your Karmic Path: Your spiritual beliefs/worldview and your home life are intimately connected. You should strive to incorporate the two areas of your life in a way that is mutually satisfying and also of benefit to children or other people who share your domestic life.

Strength: Dedication to your beliefs is your greatest strength.

Challenge: Adjusting your priorities may be an issue in your relationship.

FIFTH HOUSE/TENTH HOUSE COUPLE

Your Karmic Path: Your creativity and your career are bound together. If you pursue one at the expensive of the other, then the challenges in your relationship deepen.

Strength: Your strength lies in your strong creative talents and ambition.

Challenge: Both partners need to have equal say in the creativity/career area.

SIXTH HOUSE/ELEVENTH HOUSE COUPLE

Your Karmic Path: Through your daily work together, you help each other achieve your individual dreams. You are each other's support system and find other groups that share your visions and interests.

Strength: Commitment to an ideal is your greatest strength.

Challenge: Making your ideals a part of your daily life may be an issue in this relationship.

SEVENTH HOUSE/TWELFTH HOUSE COUPLE

Your Karmic Path: Any path involving the eighth or twelfth house is especially challenging. As a couple, you must strive for equality, where neither partner sacrifices personal power.

Strength: Your strength lies in your inner wisdoms as a couple.

Challenge: Finding the right balance between your partnership and your commitment to an exploration of your unconscious may be a challenge.

EIGHTH HOUSE/FIRST HOUSE COUPLE

Your Karmic Path: Any path involving the eighth or twelfth house is especially challenging. As a couple, you must strive to incorporate transformative events and experiences into your self-expression.

Strength: Psychic awareness is your greatest strength.

Challenge: Your challenge is to stem personal selfishness.

NINTH HOUSE/SECOND HOUSE COUPLE

Your Karmic Path: Your relationship is about integrating your personal values and worldview into a cohesive whole. Higher education, publishing, foreign countries and people, and spiritual beliefs are part of this path.

Strength: Your open minds are a source of strength.

Challenge: Strive not to become set in your ways.

TENTH HOUSE/THIRD HOUSE COUPLE

Your Karmic Path: Communication is a vital part of your profession. This could include writing, public speaking, public relations, acting, dance, or anything else that involves communication and the public.

Strength: You have a gift with words and self-expression.

Challenge: Try to integrate your career and your relationships with siblings, relatives, and neighbors in a positive way.

ELEVENTH HOUSE/FOURTH HOUSE COUPLE

Your Karmic Path: You integrate your ideals, goals, and dreams into your domestic life. Group associations and networks of people who share your ideals are important in your evolution as a couple.

Strength: You are committed to your dreams.

Challenge: You must not allow friends to interfere in your private life.

TWELFTH HOUSE/FIFTH HOUSE COUPLE

Your Karmic Path: Any path that involves the eighth or twelfth house can be challenging, but this one isn't as difficult as some of the others. As a couple, you uncover your power through your creative endeavors and children and by discovering what brings you pleasure.

Strength: Your creative drives are your greatest strength.

Challenge: Maintain equality in the relationship so that one partner doesn't sacrifice his or her creativity for the other.

Mentor

OPPOSITE SIGNS

In fairy tales, myths, movies, novels, and even dreams, the mentor archetype is depicted in any number of ways. The most common mentor archetype is an elderly man or woman who possesses magical powers. Merlin and Gandalf, for instance, essentially represent evolved hero archetypes. Another example is Dumbledore, mentor to Harry Potter and the other young magicians and wizards at Hogwarts. In the James Bond movies, Q, the weapons master, is a mentor. In *Charlies' Angels*, Charlie is a mentor.

In astrology, the mentor archetype defines couples whose signs are opposite each other, or six signs apart. Imagine a seesaw, where the point of greatest gravity shifts constantly from one end to the other. That's how the mentor archetype works in a romantic relationship. For a time, one partner plays the role of mentor, then the seesaw lowers or rises again and the other partner becomes the mentor. If the give and take doesn't exist in a mentor relationship, then the partnership probably won't last very long.

Even though a table of oppositions is included in the introduction, it's repeated here for convenience.

TABLE 8: OPPOSITIONS

Your Sun Sign	Opposite
♈ Aries	Libra
♉ Taurus	Scorpio
♊ Gemini	Sagittarius
♋ Cancer	Capricorn
♌ Leo	Aquarius
♍ Virgo	Pisces
♎ Libra	Aries
♏ Scorpio	Taurus
♐ Sagittarius	Gemini
♑ Capricorn	Cancer
♒ Aquarius	Leo
♓ Pisces	Virgo

If you're involved with someone whose Sun sign is opposite your own, be aware that some differences between you won't be resolved in this lifetime. This relationship is less about resolution than it is about learning how to integrate differences successfully into a partnership. In many ways, the mentor relationship is easier if it's between friends, business partners, siblings, or parent and child.

As a Gemini, I have had three close friends who are Sadges. One of them, Renie, was an astrologer from whom I learned some of the intricacies of astrology. Another friend, Millie, is a psychic from whom I have been getting readings for ten years. We recently wrote a book together, *Animal Totems: The Power and Prophecy of Your Animal Guides*. A third friend, Rose, is a former neighbor with whom I share a love of animals. With each of these Sadges, the mentor part of the friendship has seesawed back and forth, following its own cycles and rhythms. Sometimes they have been my mentors; other times I have been their mentors.

In a romantic partnership, though, the cycles and rhythms may be accelerated or slowed down, depending on the awareness and needs of the individuals involved. One couple I know, an Aries and a Libra, have been married for more than thirty years, have raised a family, and collaborate on writing projects and an exploration of metaphysics. They have irreconcilable differences, certainly, but they have learned how to integrate them into their marriage. In the areas where she lacks expertise, he knows the ropes, and vice versa. Each one draws on respective strengths to keep the balance in the relationship.

Sometimes in families, you find the mentor pattern repeated. My husband's parents, for instance, were a Taurus and a Scorpio, as are he and his sister. Or the oppositions in a family occur between a Sun and Moon sign or between a Sun sign and an Ascendant. In my family, my mother's Sagittarius Moon was directly opposite my Sun sign, and her Ascendant was opposite my sister's Moon sign. My husband's Sun sign and Ascendant are opposite my Ascendant. Even though Moons and Ascendants are beyond the scope of this book, these repetitive patterns within family units are often quite revealing about the larger purposes involved. Mentors always have a unique perspective and magic to share.

Sun Sign Combinations

This section describes how you and your partner relate to each other.

♈♎

ARIES/LIBRA COUPLE

They are the archetypal male and female energy, the original Adam and Eve of the zodiac. Aries, ruled by Mars, and Libra, ruled by Venus, are the polar opposites immortalized on book covers as ♂ (Mars) and ♀ (Venus). Their attraction to each other is usually quick and instinctive. Their elements, after all, mesh perfectly—fire and air.

Aries is attracted to Libra's sense of fairness and her need for balance. Libra is attracted to Aries's impulsiveness and courage. Each has qualities that the other lacks. Both are cardinal signs, so they use energy in similar ways. Both forge ahead on a singular path, blazing a trail into new territory. The territory itself differs, however, and this can be the very point where the mentor relationship is launched.

Libra's domain is people, relationships, the intellect, and social skills. The domain of Aries is wherever he deems it to be right this second. His passions lead him. Libra would love to have that sort of passion, but she has trouble making up her mind about many things; defining her passions may be as difficult as defining what she feels or thinks right this moment. Yes, it drives Aries crazy, this constant vacillation, the constant questions: "Did I do the right thing? Is it fair?" Aries doesn't think about fair and balanced; he acts from the gut.

Aries is fascinated by Libra's ability to charm anyone, anywhere, at any time. Watch her get out of a speeding ticket. Watch her charm her way into a major promotion or raise. Just watch, Aries, and study the finesse of her social skills. Aries may think of it as manipulative, but it isn't. Not manipulative, anyway, in the same sense that a Scorpio can manipulate another person. Libra has learned that to get what you want in life, charm goes further than aggression, diplomacy wins hearts, patience really is a virtue, and peace—not war—brings about change. This is how Libra mentors Aries.

When Aries acts as mentor to Libra, it's through his aggressive, take charge qualities. Aries doesn't sit around waiting for life to happen to him; he goes after what he wants. If he needs a Web site, he learns how to build one. If he needs a college scholarship, he investigates, gathers his information, and applies. If he needs a job, he goes hunting for one. His self-reliance is one of his greatest gifts.

The challenges that are likely to be encountered in a mentor relationship are twofold: Aries feels he is always right and Libra can't make up her mind; there's also the delicate balance of power within the partnership itself.

♉ ♏

TAURUS/SCORPIO COUPLE

With two fixed signs, one of the issues that surfaces rather quickly is stubbornness. Neither sign is able to surrender his or her knowledge, power, opinions, or beliefs without mulling everything over. Taurus does this through a careful culling of information and facts. Scorpio does it by testing this new information against his brilliant intuition. Taurus asks, "Is it practical?" Scorpio asks, "What's the absolute bottom line?"

When Taurus and Scorpio come together in heart, body, mind, and soul, they are a formidable team, able to start and run empires, countries, and political systems. They are able to accrue massive fortunes or begin movements that ultimately change the way people think and believe. Taurus draws on his need for pragmatism; Scorpio draws on her intuitive and research abilities.

Despite appearances to the contrary, Scorpio lacks the bull's calm patience; he is restless, unsettled, and intense. Many of his experiences and relationships are dramatic, deeply emotional, psychic, and transformative. Sometimes, he's totally confused by his own life, unable to understand why certain things have happened and what the real meaning is. But other times, he's able to seize the answers and guidance he needs through nothing other than his intuition and the sheer force of his will.

Scorpio's will, in fact, is one of his most precious commodities and it gets him through many tough spots in life. But when Taurus comes up against that will, it can be a terrifying experience. Suddenly, Taurus is confronted with a resistance as firm as concrete and as powerful as steel, a kind of Superman of the mind and psyche.

Taurus has her own resources, of course, that are every bit as terrifying to Scorpio. Scorpio admires the bull's patience and calm until it presents an obstacle to something he wants, and then he attempts to apply his will to breaking down the obstacle and finds that it doesn't work. This is always a shock to Scorpio and he must step back and regroup his energy.

The magnetism between these two polar opposites is nothing short of extraordinary. Once they meet, they are immediately aware that each holds qualities that are missing in the other. Sexually, they are evenly matched. Venus-ruled Taurus is bowled over by the emotional and intuitive intensity of Scorpio. Pluto-ruled Scorpio is astonished at Taurus's sensuality. Even when they disagree on the details of daily life (and they will), both are aware of how their differences balance their lifestyle.

The mentor qualities with these two happen in several areas. Taurus is taken with Scorpio's ability to know something with utter certainty, usually without digging for facts and figures. For Scorpio, something is either right or wrong. There aren't any gray areas. Taurus also has impeccable instincts and a highly developed intuition, but she needs facts and information to back it up. She wants what Scorpio has—passionate certainty.

Scorpio is envious of Taurus's calm, the profound depth of her solidity, dependability, and reliability. How can he develop that? How can he find that within himself? Taurus shows him the way.

♊ ⚡ ♐
GEMINI/SAGITTARIUS COUPLE

If nothing else, these two have fun together! They are entranced by each other's capacity for enjoyment, movement, adventure, and conversation. They enthusiastically engage each other in endless discussions about ideas, with Sadge offering the larger, cosmic picture and Gemini providing the minutiae. Both tend toward optimism and generally have positive attitudes about life.

In a romantic relationship, their respective independence shouldn't be a problem. If Sadge leaves for an adventure in some far-flung corner of the world, Gemini has plenty to consume himself. And the reverse is also true. When they travel together on an adventure, either the physical kind or the spiritual variety, they quickly discover that each possesses qualities the other is lacking.

Gemini secretly admires Sadge's ability to get up and go on a moment's notice. In this way, Sadge is rather like Aries, impatient to get moving. Gemini moves fast, too, but there are usually half a dozen items that require his immediate attention. "I'll catch up with you," he calls as Sadge is on her way out the door. And eventually he does, but it may not be until the next afternoon.

Sadge secretly admires the treasure trove of Gemini's knowledge. Granted, some of it is superficial knowledge, but he's so facile with language and ideas that it doesn't matter. Sadge wishes she could talk so easily about a book or a place or even a relationship. Or that she could write the way Gemini writes, the words pouring out with restless abandon.

But when Gemini acts like a mentor to Sadge, when he assumes that mantle, Sadge may balk initially and demand to know just who Gemini thinks he is, anyway. If the mentorship unfolds with more subtlety, so that Sadge thinks it's *her* idea, then Sadge simply goes with the flow. Part of the Sagittarian resistance has to do with her shadow, who thinks she has all the answers or, even worse, an edge on truth.

When Sadge acts as a mentor to Gemini, the twins are eager to absorb whatever Sadge knows, as long as Sadge doesn't get bombastic about it. Gemini will listen to just about anyone about anything unless that person is so opinionated that he or she becomes boring. Gemini can't tolerate boredom any more than Sadge can. When Sadge mentors Gemini, it often has to do with reaching for an ideal, seizing it, and living it. "Live your dream," Sadge says.

"Just one dream?" Gemini replies. "That's all I'm allowed?"

"Take it one dream at a time," advises Sadge, who rarely follows her own advice in this regard.

Thanks to Sadge's relentless search for the larger picture, she probably will recognize the past-life connections first. She may not have a word for it; the recognition may be nothing more than a feeling. But if Sadge recognizes it, Gemini will label it. Then again, maybe it will be the reverse. When two mutable signs are involved, nothing is cast in stone.

Both signs are quick-witted, but Sadge can be blunt to the point of hurtful, and that won't go over well with Gemini. Like fellow air sign Libra, Gemini prefers diplomacy, so that may be part of his mentorship of Sadge. Gemini doesn't always recognize the difference between ideas, which he possesses in abundance, and ideals, which Sadge possesses in abundance, so learning these differences from each other may be part of their mutual mentorship as well.

Regardless of whether the Gemini/Sagittarius relationship lasts for a day or a lifetime, one thing is certain: It won't ever be boring.

♋ ♑
CANCER/CAPRICORN COUPLE

Opposition is merely a term that astrology has given to signs that lie 180 degrees apart. It doesn't mean that the relationship between these signs has to be oppositional. It also can be complementary. But you may have a difficult time convincing Cancer and Capricorn of this fact.

Initially, these two react to each other in one of two ways: They either dislike each other on sight or the visceral tug is so strong that they hurl all caution to the wind and become lovers. One Capricorn woman, upon meeting a Cancer man for the first time, said, "I don't know what happened. We just hit it off at such a gut level that we ended up going to a motel."

This is a major shift for a Saturn-ruled Capricorn, who tends to stick to the tried and true, the straight and narrow, rarely leaping before she's very certain what lies on the other side. But sometimes, Capricorn simply has to bust free of the restrictions that heavy-handed Saturn places on her life, and Cancer can be the trigger that allows her to do it.

Moon-ruled Cancer lives in the most subjective of worlds. His experiences are filtered through a subjective lens, and when he comes up against formidable Capricorn, he may be struck mute. Or he may feel the same deep, inexplicable sexual attraction that the Capricorn woman did upon meeting the Cancer man. Cancer is softer than Capricorn, at least in the sense that his world is a flowing river of emotions, intuition, imagination, and visions, and Capricorn immediately recognizes this.

One area where these two have striking differences revolves around home life versus professional life. Cancer rules the home, personal environment, family, and Mom (or her equivalent); Capricorn rules the professional life, the public, career, and authority. This isn't to say that all Cancers are homebodies or that all Capricorns are married to their careers. But most Cancers do have deep feelings about their home, real estate, family, and parents, and most Capricorns do have professional interests. In a romantic relationship, a possible point of conflict can develop if so much emphasis is put on home or career that one of the partners feels ignored.

Quite often, past-life connections between these two are recognized quickly by one of the partners, probably Cancer, who tends to be the more intuitive of the two. But if the notion is foreign to Capricorn (which it may be) or if Capricorn's religious faith doesn't allow for a belief in reincarnation (also possible), then Cancer will keep this knowledge to himself and explore it on his own. Cancer is the less likely of the two to follow an organized religion. His spiritual beliefs usually have evolved over the years into something that is highly personal, whereas Capricorn may adhere to a more conventional religious structure. Both types of spirituality can be integrated into the partnership and this could be one area where the mentorship aspect manifests itself first.

Another area of possible mentorship with these two is setting goals, something Capricorn generally does very well. Then there's the softness and sensitivity that Capricorn learns from Cancer and the directness that

Cancer learns from Capricorn… You can see where this is going, right? In an ideal situation, the seesaw between these two constantly shifts—rising, falling, and rising again.

♌ ♒
LEO/AQUARIUS COUPLE

As fire and air signs, these two would seem to have a lot going for them. Air feeds fire, and fire needs oxygen to exist. Both signs are fixed, so they are stubborn when they need to be and stick to their own opinions unless convinced otherwise. But their essential differences are significant. And with these two, it certainly is true that opposites attract!

Let's take a closer look. Leo has a great deal of pride that stems from a fundamental need for approval. This alone could explain why so many Leos are attracted to the dramatic arts. After all, where else can you get such a huge and immediate dose of approval than on stage? Aquarius isn't interested in applause. He's interested in how everything works—people, computers, time, reality—it's all fair game for the idiosyncratic Aquarian intellect.

Just when Leo figures she's in charge in the relationship, Aquarius convinces her to do something totally outrageous; then she wonders whether anyone is in charge. Aquarius doesn't worry about such things. It makes no difference to him whether Leo is in charge or aliens from Pluto are in charge. He just wants to be free to pursue his interests and passions. There's a humanitarian lurking in that quirky Aquarius personality, though, and Leo can relate to that aspect of the water bearer. Leo, too, has a bleeding heart, especially when it comes to children.

But the rest of the time, Leo isn't at all sure what to make of all the rules that Aquarius breaks, as well as his lack of vanity, fascination with the future, and emotional detachment. Aquarius is equally perplexed by Leo's dramatic and emotional displays, as well as her pride, perpetual optimism, and unerring ability to turn even the worst situations to her own advantage. These areas are ripe for mentorship, but that aspect of the relationship will have to unfold on its own. Neither of these fixed signs tolerates having anything thrust on him or her, particularly with a partner.

It's not as if either of them will be able to demand that the other listen up. Leo and Aquarius either get it or they don't.

When they do get it, this relationship holds many surprises, twists, and turns, like a plot in a thriller novel. Each one is kept guessing about the other. The air of mystery and intrigue can be maddening at times for both of them, but at the heart of it, neither one would have it any other way. After all, if life can't have a few glorious and magnificent surprises, then what's the point?

♍♓

VIRGO/PISCES COUPLE

The mutual gentleness inherent in this combination is enhanced if either partner has a Moon, a Venus, or an Ascendant in the other's Sun sign. Even without the other contacts, though, Virgo and Pisces gently provide what the other lacks.

Mercury-ruled Virgo is practical, efficient, and organized. Neptune-ruled Pisces is ephemeral, psychic, imaginative, and, thanks to the co-rulership of Jupiter, able to grasp the larger picture. But Pisces, being an emotional, intuitive sign, grasps the bigger picture through her feelings. Virgo can see the trees in the forest; Pisces sees the forest. These two complement each other in ways that even they can see. But getting into a relationship at all may be the first hurdle for Virgo and Pisces. Virgo is essentially a loner who doesn't give her heart away easily. Pisces is a romantic who is all too willing to give her heart away—and often gives it away to the wrong person.

But let's say that they meet and the miraculous happens. They fall for each other. Now what? Virgo quickly learns to admire the way the fish grasps ideas without having to analyze them to death. And Pisces admires the way Virgo connects the dots through analysis. Virgo, who sometimes longs to burst free of her organization and self-criticism, secretly admires that Pisces, despite her disorganization, always seems to know where she stands in the larger scheme of things. Because Virgo and Pisces are mutable signs, they won't mind being told that the above areas are ripe for mentorship.

With these two, there shouldn't be any major quarrels about who's in charge. It's not that big a deal for either of them. Besides, their roles change constantly, so today's boss may be tomorrow's understudy. The point is that in Pisces, Virgo has the opportunity to discover how to let go and trust a power higher than herself. Whether she calls it God, the higher self, All That Is, or something else, it amounts to the same thing—faith in the unseen. In Virgo, Pisces has the opportunity to discover that the conscious mind can be just as powerful as the unconscious, intuitive mind in creating your own reality.

Together, these two have the ability and power to engage both sides of their brains. What Pisces can imagine and intuit, Virgo can verbalize and make practical. What Virgo can think, Pisces can feel. When Pisces can't make up his mind about something, Virgo can step in and point out the missing connections. When Virgo becomes too critical of self or others, Pisces can mend the rifts and make things whole again.

These two are about comfort and discernment, empathy and camaraderie. In the end, they both play for keeps.

Sun/North Node
Connections

T he descriptions below address both variations of a combination. If you have a first house Sun and your partner's North Node falls in your seventh house, or if your Sun is in the seventh house and your partner's North Node falls in your first house, then the first description applies to both.

The Sun/North Node combinations describe your karmic path as a couple—the strengths and challenges you face in the relationship and how you and your partner evolve through the partnership to achieve your individual potentials. However, you can apply the descriptions to anyone in your life.

When astrologers compare a couple's chart, they often use a biwheel, with one partner's chart in the inner wheel and the other person's chart in the outer wheel, just like we practiced at the beginning of part two. This enables you to see where your partner's planets fall in your houses and which of your planets are hit. The ways in which your partner's planets impact yours describes what your partner brings to the relationship. When your partner's chart is in the inner wheel and yours is in the biwheel, it indicates what you bring to your partner in the relationship. Always start with your natal Sun, which is the basic archetype of who you are.

By now, you've either downloaded your and your partner's charts from the Internet or have used one of the blank charts in the back of the book to place your Sun and North Node and those of your partner in the appropriate houses. However, with the opposition combinations, we have an additional component: the South Node.

Use one of the blank charts at the back of the book and follow along with this example. Seeing it will make it much easier to apply to your own life. Let's say you have a Sun in Virgo in the fourth house and that your partner has a North Node in Pisces. Draw your Sun in Virgo—☉♍—in the fourth house and put your partner's North Node in Pisces—☊♓—in your tenth house. Label it with your partner's name, so you don't get confused or place it in the outer circle of the tenth house. Now, if your partner's North Node is in Pisces, that means that his or her South Node is in the opposite sign—Virgo. Place that—☋♍—in the fourth house along with your Sun.

Any time I see this configuration in comparison charts—where one person's Sun and the partner's South Node are in the same sign (conjunct)—I know I'm looking at a past-life relationship. In natal charts, of course, we have degrees for everything; the closer the degree, the closer the karmic connection.

Common astrological wisdom says that a Sun/South Node relationship feels so comfortable and familiar it's like curling up together by a fire on a cold night. Common wisdom often advises you to run immediately in the opposite direction because neither partner will grow beyond the parameters already established in past lives. But this is where I diverge from common wisdom.

People who have known each other in past lives and share this Sun and South Node connection may come together for a variety of reasons. Perhaps this time around, their relationship is intended to be a haven that roots them and allows them to venture out to explore other areas. Or maybe the relationship serves as a spiritual boost that kicks them onto a new path or a new exploration. Sometimes, the relationship emphasizes a pattern that is holding them back in some way. The mentorship aids them in seeing the pattern and changing it.

When my daughter was in middle school, she learned that friendship isn't about bending over backward to accommodate people. Her mentor was a classmate, a girl Megan considered to be a close friend, but who was manipulative and somewhat mean-spirited. This girl also mentored Megan on clothes, hairstyles, makeup, and guys, the usual teen stuff. When I finally did the girl's chart, I realized the main issues in their friendship were related to a past life. Once Megan learned what she was supposed to learn from her friend, the friendship pretty much faded away.

In the chart below, you can see Megan's sixth house Virgo Sun (8 degrees)—☉8♍—and her friend's Virgo South Node (7 degrees) —☋7♍. The fact that Megan's Sun and the girl's South Node were in the sixth house in Megan's chart indicates that the issues occurred in Megan's daily work life, which for her was her daily school life.

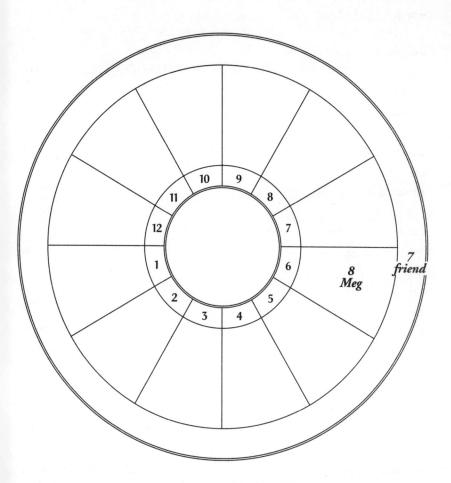

FIRST HOUSE/SEVENTH HOUSE COUPLE

Your Karmic Path: With this configuration, you have a first or seventh house Sun and your partner's North Node falls opposite your Sun. It means your partner's South Node is conjunct your Sun. The path in this relationship is to support each other's self-expression and integrate your individual visions into your partnership. You have dealt with these issues in other lives and the secret to resolving them is to confront them honestly, as a team.

Strength: Your commitment to each other is the bottom line.

Challenge: Selfishness may be a problem.

SECOND HOUSE/EIGHTH HOUSE COUPLE

Your Karmic Path: This configuration means you have a second or eighth house Sun and your partner's North Node falls opposite your Sun. It also means your partner's South Node is conjunct your Sun. Your karmic path is to share your resources with each other in a fair and equitable way. Your individual personal values also come into play. Together, you may explore areas such as reincarnation, life after death, and other metaphysical topics.

Strength: Your adventurous spirit as a team prompts you to explore areas together that you might not explore alone.

Challenge: Money and proprietary issues may surface from time to time. Deal with them honestly and directly. An example of this challenge might be when one partner insists on a prenuptial contract before getting married.

THIRD HOUSE/NINTH HOUSE COUPLE

Your Karmic Path: With this configuration, you have either a third or a ninth house Sun and your partner's North Node falls opposite your Sun. This means your partner's South Node is conjunct your Sun. Your karmic path as a couple is to communicate your worldview, spirituality, and philosophical beliefs. This may be done through writing, publishing, the law, or even foreign travel. Siblings, relatives, and neighbors play a part in your lives.

Strength: Your strong communication skills help you define your personal myths.

Challenge: If your worldviews are radically different, it could be a source of conflict in the partnership.

FOURTH HOUSE/TENTH HOUSE COUPLE

Your Karmic Path: You have either a fourth or a tenth house Sun and your partner's North Node is opposite your sun. This means that your partner's South Node is conjunct your Sun. Your karmic path as a couple is to balance your personal and professional lives in a way that is mutually satisfactory. When this path involves children, issues surface that revolve around the role each parent plays. Who is the primary caretaker? Who is the primary wage earner? One or both of you could have a home office.

Strength: Commitments to home and career are important to both of you.

Challenge: Conflicts may surround the importance of home life versus career, and vice versa.

FIFTH HOUSE/ELEVENTH HOUSE COUPLE

Your Karmic Path: You have either a fifth or an eleventh house Sun and your partner's North Node is opposite your Sun, so his or her South Node is conjunct your Sun. Your karmic path involves networking with people whose creative interests and passions support your own, but without allowing other people to dictate your creative expression. It's a challenging path because the fifth house also involves children, romance, and what you do for pleasure. Part of your karmic path as a couple may be to learn how not to be distracted by continual flirtations and romances outside your relationship.

Strength: Friends and networks of acquaintances are important to you and provide emotional and creative support.

Challenge: You need to maintain the integrity of your creative expression.

SIXTH HOUSE/TWELFTH HOUSE COUPLE

Your Karmic Path: Your Sun falls in either the sixth or the twelfth house and your partner's North Node falls opposite your Sun. This mean that your partner's South Node is conjunct your Sun. Your path is to reclaim power you have disowned over the course of your life and to integrate it into your daily work routine and daily health practices.

Strength: Your intuitive ability helps you make the right choices in your daily work life.

Challenge: Strive to resist escapism.

REAL LIFE

S everal years ago, a woman I have known for years was in town and
I realized I didn't have her chart in my database. I asked whether I
could do her chart. She seemed rather hesitant, then blurted, "But
the Catholic Church says astrology is a sin!"

I was struck mute by her response. As a long-lapsed Catholic, I
honestly didn't have any idea whether the Catholic Church deemed the
practice or use of astrology a sin. What floored me was that she actually
believed it. Once I recovered enough to say something, I explained that
astrology was a tool for self-knowledge. Why would anyone eliminate a
tool without first finding out whether it worked?

She rose to the challenge, of course, and once I explained what was
in her chart, she agreed that it was useful, then proceeded to give me the
birth data on other people in her family.

Dogma in any guise, be it religious, intellectual, or political, is
something you'll come up against time and again where astrology is
concerned. Religious pundits will declare that it's sinful or the devil's work.
Intellectual snobs will sniff with indignation and let you know that only
morons put any credence in astrology. In some towns, the practice of
astrology is lumped under a law that applies to fortunetellers and you have
to have a license to practice it.

When I run into this sort of resistance, my reaction depends on the situation. If I know the person, I usually toss down the gauntlet. "Let me show you how it works," I say. But if I don't know the person well, I just shrug and let it go. That said, though, I don't hide my interests. When my daughter brings friends home whom I've never met, I ask what signs they are. It helps me get a handle on who they are and, because I'm aware of what's going on with the daily motion of the planets, I also get a better sense of things that may be going on in their lives. Most kids are eager about anything that addresses their concerns and are hungry for information that illuminates who they are.

With new acquaintances, I often find myself looking for clues to their Sun signs in the way they talk, what they talk about, and how they dress and act. And when I have a sense of them, I ask whether they are such and such a sign. I go through spells where I'm right on, as well as spells when I'm dead wrong. Some people live the archetype of their Sun signs so closely that all it takes to peg them is a mannerism or a remark.

But other people seem to live more fully in their emotions—the archetype of their Moon signs—or according to the sign on their Ascendant. People who have a concentration of planets in one or two houses may project the archetypes of those houses more strongly than they do their Sun signs. We are complex beings in a complex world, and the way we use our potential is unique to each of us. That's why a couple who has everything in their favor may not stay together forever, or why a couple who seems to have very little in common—either in life or in their charts—stays married for fifty years.

In the end, though, it probably all comes down to free will. How hard are you willing to work at making a relationship a success without compromising your integrity and your own dreams and desires?

OTHER CONTACT POINTS

In comparing the charts of a couple, astrologers look for many other points of contact that describe the nature of the relationship. The first thing to look for in comparing your chart with a partner's is conjunctions—when your partner's Sun, Moon, Ascendant, or other planets are within four or five degrees of your Sun, Moon, Ascendant, or other planets.

On the next page are Chart 3 for actress Susan Sarandon and her partner, actor and director Tim Robbins. Their charts are compatible for many reasons, beginning with the signs on their respective Ascendants—they both have Capricorn rising. Sarandon's is at 29 degrees, 26 minutes Capricorn (29♑26), and Robbins's is at 9 degrees, 18 minutes Capricorn (9♑18). The Ascendant is the doorway to the chart, the place where we literally enter this life, and having the same sign rising provides an immediate camaraderie. Capricorn rising indicates that both are builders. Whether they are building a family or careers, they are careful, goal-oriented people who assume responsibility willingly and work hard to achieve their dreams. They walk their talk.

Both have a Libra Sun, which falls in the lovers category. This indicates that their self-expression follows the same archetype: They are diplomatic people who seek mediation and balance, fairness and justice. Sarandon and Robbins are both pacifists who are outspoken critics of the Bush administration's policies and of the war in Iraq. They are AIDS activists. They are outspoken against the death penalty. All of this is right in line with the Libra archetype.

The roles they tackle in movies—from *Dead Man Walking*, which Robbins directed and for which Sarandon won an Oscar, to *Mystic River*, for which Robbins won a Golden Globe—reflect their politics and beliefs. Sarandon's Libra Sun falls in the eighth house, indicating that she shares her resources. One example of this is that she lends her name to causes in which she believes. Robbins's Sun falls in his ninth house, suggesting that his worldview is extremely important to him. Because his North Node is also in this house, it suggests that he must express his worldview and beliefs in some way.

Emotionally, Sarandon and Robbins are quite different. Sarandon's Moon in Capricorn, at 26 degrees—26♑☽—falls within three degrees of her Capricorn Ascendant. The natal Moon on or close to the Ascendant increases your chances for fame. With a Capricorn Moon, you need structure of some kind to feel emotionally secure, are disciplined and responsible, and usually don't wear your heart on your sleeve.

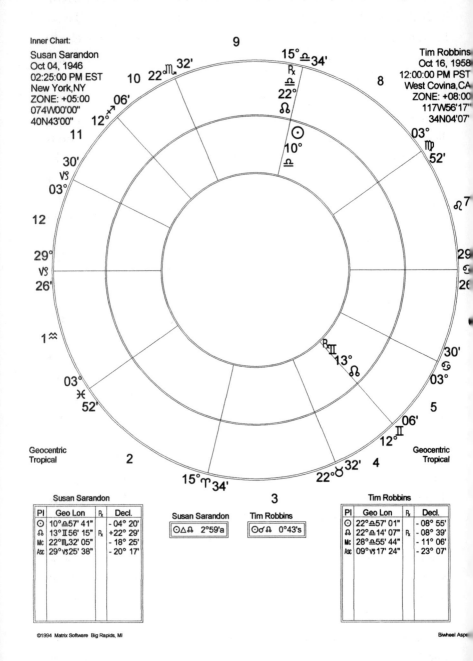

Inner Chart:

Susan Sarandon
Oct 04, 1946
02:25:00 PM EST
New York,NY
ZONE: +05:00
074W00'00"
40N43'00"

Tim Robbins
Oct 16, 1958
12:00:00 PM PST
West Covina,CA
ZONE: +08:00
117W56'17"
34N04'07"

Geocentric
Tropical

Geocentric
Tropical

Susan Sarandon

Pl	Geo Lon	Rx	Decl.
☉	10°≏57' 41"		- 04° 20'
☊	13° Ⅱ 56' 15"	Rx	+22° 29'
Mc	22°♏,32' 05"		- 18° 25'
Asc	29° ♑ 25' 38"		- 20° 17'

Susan Sarandon	Tim Robbins
☉△☊ 2°59'a	☉♂☊ 0°43's

Tim Robbins

Pl	Geo Lon	Rx	Decl.
☉	22°≏57' 01"		- 08° 55'
☊	22°≏14' 07"	Rx	- 08° 39'
Mc	28°≏55' 44"		- 11° 06'
Asc	09° ♑ 17' 24"		- 23° 07'

©1994 Matrix Software Big Rapids, MI

Biwheel Aspe

230

Robbins's Moon is in Sagittarius—♐18☽—in the twelfth house. The Sadge Moon needs emotional freedom and independence. Emotionally, he's looking for the larger truth, the bigger picture. His politics definitely reflect this. With the twelfth house placement, he's exceptionally intuitive, can be blunt, and works well behind the scenes.

Now take a look at the first biwheel chart. Sarandon's chart is on the inner wheel, and the planets in the outer wheel are those of Robbins. They illustrate some intriguing connections between them. His Sadge Moon is within five degrees of her South Node in Sadge—☋13♐—in the eleventh house. This certainly points to a past-life connection, a mentor relationship. His Sun—☉22♎—and his North Node, also at 22 degrees Libra—fall within three degrees of Sarandon's Mercury—☿25♎—in the ninth house. Mercury represents the conscious mind and communication. They communicate well and their worldviews are similar. In fact, her ideas, her mind, and the way she communicates are in line with Robbins's karmic path.

They also have another Mercury connection. His Mercury is at 0 degrees Scorpio—☿00♏—and falls within one degree of her Jupiter— ♃1♎. She expands his communication abilities and his venues for communication, and he is consciously supportive of her higher aspirations. A Mercury in Scorpio brings great intensity to communication abilities, which is certainly evident in Robbins's most recent performance in *Mystic River*.

The romantic commitment in their relationship is seen in the connection between his Venus and her Sun. His Venus in Libra—♀16♎—is within six degrees of her Sun. This conjunction, though wide, is one of the indicators of romantic compatibility in a couple.

Another intriguing connection between them is his Neptune at 4 degrees Scorpio—♆4♏—and her Mars at 6 degrees Scorpio—♂6♏. Neptune symbolizes higher inspiration, and Mars symbolizes our physical and sexual energy. A conjunction between these two suggests that Sarandon is inspired by Robbins's ideals.

Now skip down the biwheel a bit to the seventh house. In the inner wheel, you'll see Sarandon's Vertex at 1 degree Virgo—Vtx1♍—and Robbins's Pluto at 3 degrees Virgo—♇3♍. The Vertex is considered a point that means "destined encounters," agreements we make with others before we're born. When it's conjunct Pluto, in the seventh house of partnerships, it indicates a powerful and transformative relationship with roots that remain in other lives. It also suggests a powerful partnership. Robbins's Vertex at 18 degrees Leo—Vtx18♌— is also conjunct Sarandon's Pluto, but at a wider angle, six degrees. Even so, it's a kind of confirmation of the closer conjunction.

Robbins's Uranus at 15 degrees Leo—♅15♌—is within a three-degree conjunction of Sarandon's Pluto. This could indicate that he brings genius and a respect for individuality to their relationship. Other connections exist in their chart, but the conjunctions are the most powerful.

Astrologers use other methods to determine the nature of a couple's relationship. Most of them combine the two charts through various techniques, thus creating a horoscope for the relationship itself. A lengthy discussion of these techniques is beyond the scope of this book, but the section that follows provides pointers on how to interpret conjunctions between your planets and those of a partner.

READING PATTERNS

Always begin with your chart in the inner wheel and place your partner's planets in the outer wheel. Start simple, by looking just for conjunctions, as we did with the Sarandon/Robbins chart, and count only the planets that are within six degrees of your own.

If you glance back at the Sarandon biwheel, for example, you'll see that she and Robbins have a connection by sign between his Jupiter and her Venus in Scorpio. Both planets are in Scorpio. But Robbins's Jupiter in Scorpio—♃7♏—is separated by fifteen degrees from Sarandon's Venus in Scorpio—♀23♏. They're too wide to count as a conjunction.

Interpret the conjunctions according to the nature of the planets and the house placements. For easy reference about the simplified meanings of the planets and the houses, use Tables 9 and 10.

Begin by applying these simplified meanings to the planets and houses. The most important connections are those between your and your

TABLE 9: WHAT THE PLANETS REPRESENT

Planet		Meaning
AS	Ascendant	Doorway to the chart, your public mask, how others see you.
☉	Sun	Self-expression, where you shine
☽	Moon	Emotions, intuition, Mom, the inner you
☿	Mercury	Conscious mind, communication, travel
♀	Venus	Romance, love, women, the arts, yin energy
♂	Mars	Physical and sexual energy, aggression, yang energy
♃	Jupiter	Expansion, luck, success, creativity, higher mind, religious & spiritual beliefs, growth, foreign countries and cultures
♄	Saturn	Responsibilities, rules of physical reality, discipline, karma
♅	Uranus	Individuality, genius, breaks with tradition, sudden and unexpected change
♆	Neptune	Higher inspiration, visionary self, illusions, spiritual insights
♇	Pluto	Transformation, regeneration, permanent change, power, what's hidden
☊	North Node	Path to strive toward in this life
☋	South Node	Accretions of habits and attitudes from previous lives, comfort zones
Vtx	Vertex	A point that describes "destined encounters"
⊗	Path to Fortune	An Arabic part that indicates your pot of gold

partner's Sun, Moon, and Ascendant. A Sun/Moon connection (you understand your partner's emotions) and a Moon/Moon connection (you're in synch emotionally with your partner) are also significant.

In terms of past-life connections, look for contacts from either of the Nodes or the Vertex to any of the planets. The house placement will describe the area of life where this influence in felt most strongly.

If, for example, you and your partner share contacts between the Moon and Pluto in the seventh house, then the simplified meaning might be that the emotional connection between you is both intuitive and powerful. But it could also indicate a power struggle in which one partner tries to control the other. If the connection falls in the fifth house, then there may be a power struggle about children and/or creative projects, or you might bolster and support each other's creativity. Use your intuition in the interpretations.

The Part of Fortune is the most common Arabic part (of dozens) used by Western astrologers. It's the equivalent of the pot of gold in your astrological lineup. By sign and house placement, it describes opportunities that come to you and the events and situations that bring you joy.

Look at the individual charts for Sarandon and Robbins. Her Part of Fortune falls in her third house, in Taurus. She's interested in ideas and the mental process and enjoys communicating in relationships. She seeks things that are stable, enduring, and worthy.

Robbins's Part of Fortune is in Pisces, in his second house. His pot of gold lies in discovering and understanding his true values. He's generally fortunate where money is concerned, but only if he stays in line with his deepest and most genuine beliefs and values. He's intuitive (Pisces) about money and financial opportunities and is in tune with something much larger than himself.

To interpret your Path of Fortune, just assign the meaning of the sign and the house placement to it.

There are also critical angles in a chart—the Ascendant, the cusp of the fourth house, the cusp of the seventh house, and the cusp of the tenth house. Any time your partner's planets hit these points in your chart, it's particularly significant.

TABLE 10: HOUSE MEANINGS

House	Meaning
First	You (versus others); your self-expression, social mask, physical appearance, general state of physical health
Second	Money, possessions, earning power, attitudes about money, personal values
Third	Communication, conscious mind, siblings, relatives, neighbors, neighborhood, short journeys
Fourth	Your home and personal environment, your most private self, the foundation of who you are, your roots, real estate, emotional security, the nurturing parent
Fifth	Creativity, children, pleasure, romance, speculation, small animals
Sixth	Daily health and work, volunteer activities
Seventh	Intimate partnerships, marriage, business partnerships, open enemies, contracts
Eighth	Your instincts, shared resources, metaphysics, transformative experiences, taxes, death, insurance, sexuality
Ninth	Higher mind, your philosophy, religious or spiritual beliefs, foreign travel, countries and cultures, your worldview
Tenth	Your career, profession, external achievements
Eleventh	Friends, ambitions, the people you hang with, dreams, networking
Twelfth	Your personal unconscious, what's hidden or behind the scenes, power we've disowned

APPENDIX

NORTH NODE EPHEMERIS

May 10, 1899—Jan 21, 1901	Sagittarius
Jan 22, 1901—July 21, 1902	Scorpio
July 22, 1902—Jan 15, 1904	Libra
Jan 16, 1904—Sep 18, 1905	Virgo
Sep 19, 1905—Mar 30, 1907	Leo
Mar 31, 1907—Sep 27, 1908	Cancer
Sep 28, 1908—Mar 23, 1910	Gemini
Mar 24, 1910—Dec 8, 1911	Taurus
Dec 9, 1911—June 6, 1913	Aries
June 7, 1913—Dec 3, 1914	Pisces
Dec 4, 1914—May 31, 1916	Aquarius
June 1, 1916—Feb 13, 1918	Capricorn
Feb 14, 1918—Aug 15, 1919	Sagittarius
Aug 16, 1919—Feb 7, 1921	Scorpio
Feb 8, 1921—Aug 23, 1922	Libra
Aug 24, 1922—Apr 23, 1924	Virgo
Apr 24, 1924—Oct 26, 1925	Leo
Oct 27, 1925—Apr 16, 1927	Cancer
Apr 17, 1927—Dec 28, 1928	Gemini
Dec 29, 1928—July 7, 1930	Taurus
July 8, 1930—Dec 28, 1931	Aries
Dec 29, 1931—June 24, 1933	Pisces
June 25, 1933—Mar 8, 1935	Aquarius
Mar 9, 1935—Sep 14, 1936	Capricorn
Sep 15, 1936—Mar 3, 1938	Sagittarius
Mar 4, 1938—Sept 12, 1939	Scorpio
Sep 13, 1939—May 24, 1941	Libra
May 25, 1941—Nov 21, 1942	Virgo
Nov 22, 1942—May 11, 1944	Leo
May 12, 1944—Dec 13, 1945	Cancer
Dec 14, 1945—Aug 2, 1947	Gemini
Aug 3, 1947—Jan 26, 1949	Taurus
Jan 27, 1949—July 26, 1950	Aries
July 27, 1950—Mar 28, 1952	Pisces
Mar 29, 1952—Oct 9, 1953	Aquarius
Oct 10, 1953—Apr 2, 1955	Capricorn
Apr 3, 1955—Oct 4, 1956	Sagittarius
Oct 5, 1956—June 16, 1958	Scorpio

June 17, 1958—Dec 15, 1959	Libra
Dec 16, 1959—June 10, 1961	Virgo
June 11, 1961—Dec 23, 1962	Leo
Dec 24, 1962—Aug 25, 1964	Cancer
Aug 26, 1964—Feb 19, 1966	Gemini
Feb 20, 1966—Aug 19, 1967	Taurus
Aug 20, 1967—Apr 19, 1969	Aries
Apr 20, 1969—Nov 2, 1970	Pisces
Nov 3, 1970—Apr 27, 1972	Aquarius
Apr 28, 1972—Oct 27, 1973	Capricorn
Oct 28, 1973—July 10, 1975	Sagittarius
July 11, 1975—Jan 7, 1977	Scorpio
Jan 8, 1977—July 5, 1978	Libra
July 6, 1978—Jan 12, 1980	Virgo
Jan 13, 1980—Sep 24, 1981	Leo
Sep 25, 1981—Mar 16, 1983	Cancer
Mar 17, 1983—Sep 11, 1984	Gemini
Sep 12, 1984—Apr 6, 1986	Taurus
Apr 7, 1986—Dec 2, 1987	Aries
Dec 3, 1987—May 22, 1989	Pisces
May 23, 1989—Nov 18, 1990	Aquarius
Nov 19, 1990—Aug 1, 1992	Capricorn
Aug 2, 1992—Feb 1, 1994	Sagittarius
Feb 2, 1994—July 31, 1995	Scorpio
Aug 1, 1995—Jan 25, 1997	Libra
Jan 26, 1997—Oct 20, 1998	Virgo
Oct 21, 1998—Apr 9, 2000	Leo
Apr 10, 2000—Oct 12, 2001	Cancer
Oct 13, 2001—Apr 13, 2003	Gemini
Apr 14, 2003—Dec 25, 2004	Taurus
Dec 26, 2004—June 21, 2006	Aries
June 22, 2006—Dec 18, 2007	Pisces
Dec 19, 2007—Aug 21, 2009	Aquarius
Aug 22, 2009—Mar 3, 2011	Capricorn
Mar 4, 2011—Aug 29, 2012	Sagittarius
Aug 30, 2012—Feb 18, 2014	Scorpio
Feb 19, 2014—Nov 11, 2015	Libra
Nov 12, 2015—May 9, 2017	Virgo
May 10, 2017—Nov 6, 2018	Leo
Nov 7, 2018—May 4, 2020	Cancer
May 5, 2020—Jan 18, 2022	Gemini
Jan 19, 2022—July 17, 2023	Taurus
July 18, 2023—Jan 11, 2025	Aries

YOUR JOURNEY

If you continue your journey into astrology, there are dozens of terrific Web sites that provide lots of diverse information. Here are some of my favorites:

www.12house.com
Astrologer Mark S. Husson features a fascinating roundup of articles on various types of astrology. You can subscribe at a reasonable price and obtain free charts and other goodies.

www.accessnewage.com
This site belongs to Robert Hand, probably one of the best astrologers in the world. He has information on his site you won't see anywhere else because of the nature of the astrological research he does.

www.astro.com
This site is chock-full of great information. One of its most intriguing features is astrocartography—the astrology of location. Where in the world is the best place for you to live? Find out. You can also obtain free birth charts from this site.

www.astrodatabank.com
Lois Rodden, who passed away recently, made a name for herself in the astrological world by collecting birth data from thousands of individuals and classifying the data according to its accuracy. Her site has many wonderful bits of information about astrology and people in the news. Mark McDonough, her business partner, now runs the site. They developed an invaluable piece of software, AstroDataBank, that features nearly 25,000 names with birth information and biographies. The site also reviews astrological software.

www.astrologyzone.com
Astrologer and writer Susan Miller has great stuff on her site, including a detailed monthly horoscope for each sign.

www.booktalk.com

Sally Schoenweiss started this site a number of years ago as a showcase for several writers. The site has grown tremendously and is a fascinating place for the inside scoop on publishing, writing, and authors. I do a monthly horoscope column on creativity.

www.janspiller.com

This site belongs to astrologer and writer Jan Spiller. It has great information and you get one free chart. If you subscribe for $3.95 a month, you get to download unlimited charts.

www.mceagle.com

This site is extremely unusual. Astrologer Nancy McMoneagle and her husband, Joe, feature a combination of astrology and remote viewing. Joe was psychic spy number one in the government's remote viewing project, Stargate, and Nancy is an ace astrologer!

www.moonvalleyastrologer.com

Astrologer and writer Celeste Teal has fascinating articles, predictions, and all kinds of tidbits on astrology that are useful to novices and pros alike. She has amassed fascinating information on lunar and solar eclipses, too.

www.patterns.com and www.AstroSoftware.com

These two sites sell the same product—the Kepler astrology program. You can see examples online of the various types of horoscope wheels, sample reports, and other goodies that are offered.

www.thenewage.com

This site, owned by Matrix Software, has tons of terrific information and a databank of birth data on celebrities and well-known individuals. Matrix produces great software, including WinStar Plus, which generated the charts used in this book. They also produce software on oracles, the tarot, and a host of other intriguing topics.

www.zyntara.com

This site is from the U.K. and sells software on fixed stars produced by astrologer and writer Bernadette Brady. It's fascinating to see the examples of what this software can do and the report it generates on a little understood facet of astrology.

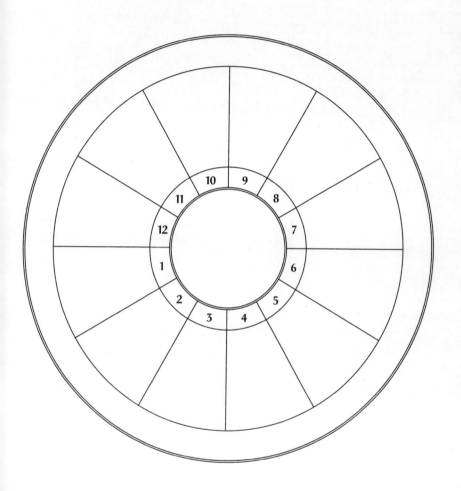

BIWHEEL CHART

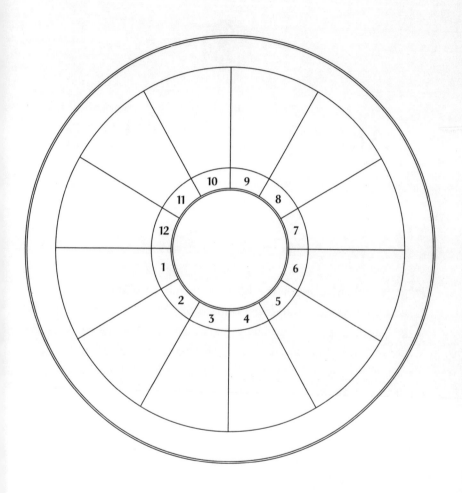

BIWHEEL CHART

ABOUT THE AUTHOR

T rish MacGregor has been practicing astrology for more than twenty years. She's the author of thirteen nonfiction books, including eight astrology books. As T.J. MacGregor, she's the author of twenty-four novels. In 2003, she won the Edgar Allan Poe award for her suspense novel *Out of Sight*. She also writes a horoscope column on creativity for writers at booktalk.com and can be contacted there at **www.booktalk.com/tjmacgregor.**